*To You Eric and Brenda
And Your House!
His Love*

My Covenant Over Your Children and Children's Children

Linda Greene

His Love Publications

**My Covenant
Over Your Children and
Children's Children**
by
Linda Greene

Copyright by
Linda Greene
2000
All right reserved

Printed in
the United States of America

Published by
His Love Publications
P.O. Box 5995
Thomasville, GA 31758

ISBN 0-9676644-5-4
Library of Congress Catalog Card Number: 99-97263

I Dedicate this Book

- To You, Heavenly Father, for the giving of your Dear Son Jesus that I and My household can have life everlasting and live in this covenant. Thank you for enlarging your written word in my heart and bringing it to the hearts and lives of many.

- To you, Charlie, My Husband, My Beloved who has loved me all these years with a sacrificial love and has allowed me to fulfill, in a wonderful way, the call of God on my life.

- To you, Trevor and Todd, my Precious sons, whom I dearly love. You have taught me so much about letting go and trusting. Through you, I have learned much of our Father's care and love as a parent. Because of you this book has been written. The words and everlasting covenant of this book are yours forever.

- To you, Cindy, my daughter-in-love, I see you like my very own daughter, sent to our family as the chosen and designated wife for our son, Todd. You are very special to me. I love you.

- To you, Landon and Aaron, my grandsons-and my future grandchildren. I loved you before you were born, and I spoke the promises of God over you while you were being formed in your mother's womb. May you receive and grow in the riches of His glorious inheritance in you. This covenant belongs to you and to your offspring.

- To you, Mama, who bore me and has loved me as only a Mother can.

In Appreciation

Ivanell Flowers
for the many long hours
she spent typing my
hand-written manuscript.

Mary Friend Shepard
for the work she did on
the punctuation.

All Scripture quoted are from the Amplified version
of the Bible unless otherwise noted.

Introduction

"Hey, Linda, God Loves You! Did you know that? He wants you! Desires You! Has always wanted you!"

So long ago, but it seems like yesterday, I just happened to open a small book. It fell open on page ninety-four. There were those words, that you see written above, with my name-right there before my eyes--I could hardly believe what I was seeing. For you see, the deep longing of my heart had always been "God, do you really love me...me, Linda?" Out of this whole world, with its billions of people--could God really know my name? Not only "Does God really love me? But does God want me? Really desire me?" Well, there it was written in this little book in black and white. I knew the words were written just for me. What I had always needed to hear and would need to hear, for the rest of my life and for all eternity. Could God really be so near? Be so personal? How could He have known the deep secret questions of my heart? I wondered, "Could the God of this whole universe have someone write these words in this little book just for me; and one day as I picked up the book cause the pages to fall open to the very words I needed so desperately to hear?"

Well, that day the seed of His personal Word to me was planted. Through the years, miraculously, the Holy Spirit worked on that which had fallen on receptive soil. As the seed, the elements and the soil have merged together in my life--I have stepped out of the world of mere words into the pure adventure of "believing with the heart," seeing the living truth of God's Love in His promises for myself.

This book has been written because of the Father's fervent desire to sow into your life these same covenant promises of His love for you. As He spoke...my heart listened...my hands wrote...

Who knows? Perhaps one day I might hear *you* say, "Hey, Linda, God loves *Me!* Did you know that? He even knows My name! He wants *Me*! Desires *Me*! Has always wanted *Me*! He has now sown these Words of His Covenant into my life and into my children and my children's children for all eternity!

How do I know this? I just happened to open ***this little book***!"

Psalm 105:8

He is mindful of HIS COVENANT and forever it is imprinted on His heart, the word which He commanded and established to a thousand generations.

Contents

My Covenant 17
Building a Sure House. 19
Write in a Book. 21
House on the Rock. 23
I Will be God of all Families. 25
I Must Stay at Your House. 27
A Lamb According to Your Families. 29
You and Your Household Shall be Saved. 31
Light in Your Dwellings. 33
Dress Your Sons and Daughters in Silver and Gold. 35
A Woman who Paid Attention. 37
There is None Righteous. 39
In Your Natal Blood. 41
This Child is Given to the Lord Forever. 43
He is Able to Keep. 45
Her Household is Doubly Clothed in Scarlet. 49
His Mother Made Him a Robe 51
No Words Shall Fall to The Ground. 54
You and Your Descendants. 55
You and Your Family Shall Come into The Ark. 57
Stones of Remembrance. 59
You Shall Let Your Children Know. 61
The Stone as a Pillow Under Your Head. 63
Five Smooth Stones. 65
The Scarlet Cord. 67
You and Your House Shall Live. 69
God Remembered His Covenant. 71
Your Children Shall Return. 73
I Will Hiss For Your Children. 75
Jesus' Prayer for Your Children. 77

In the Father's Hand	79
I Will Not Lose One of Them	81
Your Confidence is in Me	83
Bringing Forth Children Blessed of the Lord	85
I Will Save Your Children	88
The Apple of My Eye	89
I Want to be Mother Hen	91
I Desire to Gather Your Children Around Me	95
All Your Children Shall Be Taught by Me	99
Your Children and Their Offspring Shall Eat at My Table Always	101
When It Pleases God	103
I Am the Author and Source	105
I Will Pour Out My Spirit Upon Your Offspring	107
The Work of My Hands	109
I Will Deliver—You Intercede	111
I Will Give Light to You and Your Descendants	113
I Will Bring Your Sons and Daughters From Afar	115
Your Sons and Daughters Shall Prophesy	117
Have Confidence in Me Concerning Your Children	119
I Will Make for You a House	121
I Am the Builder and Furnisher	123
Except I Build the House	125
The Child Will Be a Nazarite	127
Your Children Around Your Table	131
Your Children Shall Be Established Before Me	133
My Righteousness To Your Children's Children	135
You and Your Children's Children Shall Dwell in the Land	137
Guard and Keep These Truths	139
My Majesty to Your Children	141
Your Children's Children	143
Your Children Will Not Beg for Bread	145
I Will Give Increase to You and Your Children	147

Promise of the Holy Spirit to You and Your Children 149
I Will Save You and Your Offspring. .151
Come Have Breakfast. 153
Your Sons and Daughters Shall Be Recovered. 157
Your Descendants Will Be Delivered. 159
Your Children are My Heritage and My Reward. 161
Your Offspring Shall Endure Forever. 163
Companionship and Participation. 165
My Children Living in The Truth. 167
Enter Into My Joy. 169

My Covenant

As for Me, this is My Covenant with them, says the Lord; My Spirit who is upon you, and My words which I have put in your mouth, shall not depart out of your mouth, or out of the mouths of your children, or out of the mouths of your children's children, says the Lord, from henceforth and forever." Isaiah 59:21

My Beloved, how you delight Me in receiving that which was established before the foundation of the world! I had you in mind when I gave this word and I told My Holy Spirit to write it down. I knew you would see it with your heart's eyes one day and you would allow Me to sow it deep in your heart, not only to bring you rest but for all those who would hear it and see and find rest for their souls. As you noticed, I said "As For Me," in other words this is where I stand, this is My promise or pledge with you concerning your children and your children's children. I have given it, but only as you receive My pledge of love in agreement can it be ratified. You know through the years you have spoken many words, many of your own words, useless, fearful, meaningless or hurtful words. Beloved, My Words of Love, Life and Power which I have put in your mouth shall not depart out of the mouths of your children. Many times a different spirit came forth and acted and reacted which was not of Me. My Covenant with you, Dear One, *is My Spirit,* Who is within you, that shall never depart out of your children and their children henceforth and forever!

I will cause My faith to rise up within you to desire the covenant and for it to grow deep within the center of your heart. My Heart is in your heart!

Building a Sure House

Truly, does not my house stand with God? For He has made with me an Everlasting Covenant, ordered in all things and sure. For will He not cause to prosper all my help and my desire? II Samuel 23:5

I am building My house Beloved, inside you and around you. It will be a house of rest in which I may rest. So ultimately you, my bride, might rest from all our enemies; those strongholds of unbelief, fear, jealousy, resentment, disappointments and unforgiveness that would rob you, My Precious One, of My power, love and a sound mind. Oh, how I have come that I might destroy the works of the devil in your life, so that we may be truly seated together, agreeing as to how My house is being built.

You remember Dear One, as you read in Exodus— how I laid out the instructions for the building of My Tabernacle, how I did not leave one inch of it to man's discretion. As The Spirit led Moses and the skilled workers; He even led all the women in the embroidery work on the cloths. How much more precious you are to Me. As you wait before Me and listen to My word, My Holy Spirit will not be lax or behind time. Every inch will be ordered as I build My house in you, My Precious One, line upon line, precept upon precept, here a little, there a little. That which I build within you is perfect. It will not be by your might or your power, but by My Spirit. Trust Me, I truly am the author and finisher of your faith. I will build My house.

You remember the day you saw in My word how I laid out the heavens with a nine-inch span? You asked your teenage son, Todd, who works with his hands, what it meant to lay out a work and build it all with a nine-inch span. He looked at you and said "He is building VERY CAREFULLY." Oh Beloved, how much care and thought I have put in you, even before the foundation of the earth I called you by name. You are mine. I will never leave you or forsake you, or even relax My hold on you.

You know right now My Son has gone to prepare a place for you, a house just like the one I am building in you; a house of beauty, for you, yes, and for your household as I have sworn to you. All My Son is waiting on is for Me to say "Go." The house is complete, filled with My covenant, an everlasting covenant I have made with My Beloved Son.

Write in a Book

2) Thus says the Lord, the God of Israel: Write all the words that I have spoken to you in a book.
3) For, note well, The days are coming, says the Lord, when I will release from captivity My people Israel and Judah, says the Lord, and I will cause them to return to the Land that I gave their Fathers, and they will possess it. Jeremiah 30: 2 ,3

My Beloved, how your heart rejoiced years ago when you saw in My Word where I have a Book of Remembrance that I am writing with your name on it. In My Precious book is where I say you talked often with others about Me and spoke My words. At that very moment I told all of Heaven to be silent while I listened and wrote all your words in My Book of Remembrance. You should be reminded of John's writing in the Book of Revelation how Heaven will be commissioned to be silent while all the prayers through the ages that have not gone unnoticed will be poured forth from My throne room. Not one word is lost, My Dear One.

When on that day I open My Book with your name on it, I will be like a proud Papa reading his diary about his child. You will say then, "Father, when did I say thus and thus, I don't remember speaking that" and I will have the joy of bringing it to your remembrance. What brought delight to Me was when My Spirit leaped in your heart to write your Book of Remembrance for Me. I spoke and you told everything within you, your mind and emotions, to keep silent and listen only to My words and you hid them in your heart. I have told you, remind Me of My words to you, don't keep silent. For as sure as heaven and earth shall pass away only My words shall remain. I esteem My word above My name.

When I tell you to note well, to take notice, that means you can rest in it, it will take place. Notice those whom you have prayed for and entrusted to Me; I will bring them from where they are to My Land (My Heart) and they will possess the Land (the gifts and fruit of My Spirit. My very Self).

Truly, as you have opened the door of your heart and invited Me to come and dine with you, we will both have a Book of Remembrance to present to each other that will be tried and true, and though through the fire of affliction, words of gold shall come forth.

House on the Rock

24) So everyone Who hears these Words of Mine and acts upon them will be like a wise man who built his house up on the Rock.
25) And the rain fell and the floods came and the winds blew and beat against that house; Yet it did not fall because it had been founded on the Rock. Matthew 7:24-25

Beloved, there are many voices in the world, clamoring for your attention, your agreement, and your obedience. As I have said, the whole world lies under the power of the evil one, satan, who is the father of lies. He has been a liar from the very beginning. There is absolutely no truth in him. The world listens and obeys his words of fear and distrust, but you My child are mine.

As you listen to My words, My words of trust and faith, My perfect love will cast out all fear. The storms of life may come crashing down all around you, but oh my Dear One, believe My words are forever established and settled in heaven. They shall never pass away. My Son Jesus Christ, being the chief corner stone, is holding My house together. All things are being built and furnished by Him and through Him; all things are being established, even your faith. Yes, Precious One, you shall enter My rest, because you have ceased from your own labor and said in your heart, "I trust my Father, the One who is true, the One who says **trust Me**." Commit your way to Me and I will surely bring it to pass.

Yes, with My house there are no faulty cracks, no leaky roofs, no cracked windows. My house is solid with a firm foundation that shall not tilt or slide. It will still be standing when all else gives way and crumbles.

Precious One, don't try to build it with the workings of your own mind and hands. Remember how I have told you it is a foolish woman who tries to build her own house. You know how you tried and tried to help Me. All the fears behind each nail! You know we had to tear each wall out when you found out "Except the Lord build the house, they labor in vain that build it." It is painful and grievous for the moment, but oh what a house for all eternity!

My house is a home where love dwells, for I am total love and My perfect love casts out all fear. I am the *Rock* that wants to support you and your household so that no gate in Hell can prevail against you. It is a *sure* house that you can count on standing forever. My Words are everlasting!

I Will be God of all the Families

At that time, says the Lord, will I be the God of all the families of Israel, and they will be My people. Jeremiah 31:1

My child, I want My people to know how I love and care for their family. Before the foundation of the world I desired and was after a family, a family of My own. The world has lost sight of what family is today. My Word speaks of fathers, mothers, children and my way in a household that brings forth my love, joy and peace. As each family looks to Me to discover my design for them, they will be a unit of strength and love. As a pattern and example of Me they will be a good advertisement of My Heavenly Family for all eternity. There are families all over the earth. Some are bound together, but not bound together in Me. My family is bound together with Me through my covenant of love, the blood of my Dear Son, Jesus Christ, who gave His life that I might have many sons and daughters.

When Abraham was laid to rest why do you think I said in my Word "I gathered him to his people"? I likewise will gather you to yours. I am God of your family. I love those whom you love and entrust to Me.

I Must Stay at Your House

And when Jesus reached the place, He looked up and said to him, Zaccheaus, hurry and come down, for I must stay at your house today. Luke 19:5

Oh, Precious One, remember that day when I walked by and called you by name. I reached that place in your heart in a way that only I could reach. You had been looking at Me and knowing Me from afar. You really did not know Me that well, so you really couldn't trust Me at the time. You only hoped. You thought you might get intimate with Me and get to know Me in the high places of your life, maybe through more church meetings, or listening to more intellectual preachers, or even memorizing My Word. Dear One, when I surprised you and called you by name, you knew that I knew you better than yourself. Precious child, I'm the One who made you, remember?

I called you down from all those high and lofty places, places that knowledge can puff up. As My Word says "only love edifies." So I said "Please don't keep looking and listening to Me from a distance. Don't stay there one more minute. Hurry, draw near to Me. Get to know My heart, My thoughts, My ways. I want you to know My love."

My child there is only one place in this whole world that I can go to do this, and that is why I want to go *Home* with you and I want to stay there with you, where your very heart is, where all your thoughts, desires, and actions cannot hide in every closet of your life, where no one else might understand you. Remember I am the One who formed you, and called you by name, you are mine. If I live at Home in your house, when we go out your door to the other places, church, store, highways and byways of life, I'll be there. Only as I can be at home in your heart, can I be everywhere else you are.

Invite Me to come to your house and please invite Me to stay!

A Lamb According to Your Families

21) Then Moses called for all the elders of Israel, and said to them, Go forth, select and take a Lamb according to your families and kill the Passover Lamb.
27) You shall say, It is the sacrifice of the Lord's Passover, for He passed over the houses of the Israelites in Egypt when He slew the Egyptians but spared our houses. And the people bowed their heads and worshiped. Exodus 12: 21 & 27

My Beloved, back in the beginning I made provision for My families. My covenant of love was going forth then. My word was "go," do not sit still as one with no hope in all your sin. I have made a way, *A Lamb*, for all your family. Notice I said *A Lamb*. That was where all your sin and trespasses were to go, on the lamb. I passed over the houses of those who put the blood of the lamb on the outside doorposts of their houses.

Oh My child, have you ever thought what would have happened that night if all the family had gathered around the table after having selected the most choice, perfect lamb; prepared the lamb just right; had spoken of Me and My words and had sung songs into the night, but had taken the blood of the Lamb and put it in a basin and left it in the corner of the living room? Oh, everything else would have been meaningful, but the household would have been destroyed not having acted on their faith to apply the blood.

What a picture today, My Dear One, for My New Covenant where My Son, Jesus, was slain for the sins of the world. You, Precious One, must accept Him. I went forth and selected Him as the perfect sacrifice, but you must not stop there, looking at Him, talking about Him, singing about Him, reading and quoting My Word. You must apply the blood in every situation. You know how in My Word I said many in the Body of Christ are sick even unto death because they have not discerned right things pertaining to My Son's body. My Son's body was slain before the foundation of the earth for you. The blood was poured forth out of Emmanuel's veins, a fountain that never runs dry. In applying My blood through My Son to you, I gave five promises in My Covenant, My Everlasting Covenant. I want My children to look and discern My Son's Body that "bore your grief, that was wounded for your transgressions, that was bruised for your guilt and iniquities; the chastisement for your peace and well being was upon Him, and with His stripes you were healed and made whole". Yes, look and discern My Son's whole work in His body so you can believe and be whole in your body, soul and spirit.

You and Your Household Shall be Saved

Believe in the Lord Jesus Christ and you will be saved you and your household as well. Acts 16:31

My Dear One, what a promise I made! Down through the ages many have fallen asleep on their knees by their bed with these words bringing rest to their hearts. The heart is where it has to take place and grow, sometimes many years before seeing any outward sign of an inward hope. Many cries have gone up of "How long Lord, how long?", knowing in the fullness of time, I do all things well. As for Me, My way is perfect. I work and bring to pass the fulfillment of all that I have spoken to you.

If you notice I speak here, only to one person, *you*. I did not speak or make a promise to the whole household or to a person in your household. I spoke only to *you*, *Beloved*, only *you*. You chose to "stand in the gap" for your loved ones, *you* believe, present tense. Now have faith in Me to perform that which is My will, My desire; I will bring it to pass. Did you see where I say "shall be saved"? Precious One, as I told Habbakuk, "Though the promise seems to delay or tarry, wait for it." On the day of the Lord you will not be disappointed that you trusted Me and My promise. My word to you concerning My promise is true. Yes assuredly, your household shall be saved because *You* believed Me. I cannot lie.

Light in Your Dwellings

The Egyptians could not see one another, nor did anyone rise from his place for three days, but all the Israelites had natural light in their dwellings. Exodus 10:23

My Beloved as you see the world around you become darker and darker know that I will light My house within you. As I have said in My word, the path of the just shall shine more and more brightly and clearly until that perfect day. You remember years ago when I spoke to your heart and told you your steps would not be hampered, your path would be clear and open and when you run you would not stumble. I have said I am the Light of the world. You will be a Light, as you abide in My words and My words abide in you. You carry My light everywhere you go. With your mind renewed in My thoughts and My ways, you can speak to a dark area in a person and shed light abroad in a depressed or fearful heart and set a prisoner free.

Many people you meet on the street are bound on the inside in prison chains. Many with sorrowful hearts are bound with grief. My light bearer is you, Dear One. Go brighten My world. Sometimes My light is rejected seemingly for the moment, but as you shine, speaking My word of love and encouragement I am able to follow these home and continue to speak to their heart. I have said, "Comfort my people, as I have comforted you, Dear child, go and comfort. I am a Father of Light, a Father of Love." Let the hurting world be drawn to Me by your love, unconditional love, asking nothing, demanding nothing. That is Grace, My Grace, bought and paid for by My Son's blood.

My child, allow Me to live in your house and permeate your walls and windows, and the whole world which cannot see or move because of the darkness that is coming will see My light. I will give light and understanding to all the deep crevices and dark closets of your soul. As I light up your life, you will bring light and glory to Me.

Dress Your Sons and Daughters in Silver and Gold

...Every woman shall [insistently] solicit of her neighbor and of her that may be residing at her house jewels and articles of silver and gold, and garments, which you shall put on your sons and daughters, and you shall strip the Egyptians [of belongings due to you.] Exodus 3:22

Beloved, you know how as I instructed each step of the way for my children in the land of Egypt many years ago, it had spiritual implications for you now. This word is to you today. This is for every woman, not a few or one, but all who go forth and are obedient and bold to take back all that is due their sons and daughters.

My desire is for your heart to see that out of life's situations where you live, the Egyptians (the world-enemy to your soul, Satan) have long kept loved-ones, sons and daughters in bondage. Satan has blinded their eyes from seeing who they are and what they have in Me. Dear One, as a believer who trusts Me for your sons and daughters, take back all the wages the enemy has stolen from you spiritually. In your heart and mind dress these children from now on with silver and gold. The silver represents My redemption, and the gold, the fullness and Glory of all that I am in them. Dress them in those precious garments of Praise. Speak to them and tell them that as they trust Me, I am the One who delights to take off those filthy rags and put my robe of righteousness on them. Just like the Prodigal Son, I said, "Bring the Robe, bring the Ring." We rejoice because this Precious One who was dead has come to his senses of who he is. He knew to come to his Father's house.

Greatly rejoice, My Beloved in Me, let your soul exalt in God, for He has clothed you with the garments of salvation, He has covered you with the Robe of Righteousness, as a bridegroom decks himself with a garland and a bride adorns herself with her jewels. I want you to see yourself and your sons and daughters fitly dressed. Insist, I say insist that My Word of Covenant is true. I cannot deny My Words to you. Heaven and earth shall pass away but My Words shall remain forever.

Your sons and daughters are mine. I will publicly recognize and openly declare them to be My jewels (My special possession, My peculiar treasure). You can count on that.

As I have said in My Word the kingdom of God suffers violence and the violent seize it by force. With your faith seize that Silver and Gold and Jewels and Garments. Put it on your sons and daughters and as I said from the beginning, "It is the sons and daughters that will go into the promised land." My promise is for your sons and daughters to you. They shall occupy the land that I have promised and given to you.

A Woman Who Paid Attention

14) One of those who listened to us was a woman named Lydia from the city of Thyatira, a dealer in fabrics dyed in purple. She was [already] a worshiper of God, and the Lord opened her heart to pay attention to what was said by Paul.
15) And when she was baptized along with her household, she earnestly entreated us, saying, "If, in your opinion, I am One really convinced [that Jesus is the Messiah and the Author of Salvation] and that I will be faithful to the Lord, come to my house and stay." And she induced us [to do it.] Acts 16:14,15

My Dear One, that day as I spoke My Words to bring hope and life to many through my servant Paul, only one and I call her by name, Lydia paid attention to what was said. She had heard of and worshiped Me, but had not yet heard how My Son had bled and died and rose again to not only bring her eternal salvation, but her whole household. I opened her heart to pay attention. She responded and insisted my servant stay at her house. That was like insisting I come and stay there. Oh, Beloved, if you will pay attention, I will come, stay, live and talk with you at your house. I will speak and continue to speak. Just desire for me to open your heart to pay attention. *I will speak*. All your family that you are holding by faith, I will speak to and touch as I have promised.

There is None Righteous

...There is None Righteous ... No Not One.   Romans 3:10

My Precious One, when you see all your sons and daughters and you tend to think that one is more holy or righteous than another, believe it not. In one household you have children with different natures. One may seem to be more pleasant or quiet or kind; one may be more easy to please or get along with, but My Word says that all who are born come into this world unrighteous with the nature of the first Adam. Only through believing on My Son, Jesus, the last Adam, can all become righteous. I stand ready with My Robe of Righteousness to clothe all as their eyes are opened to see the filthy rags on their body.

I have that clean turban that I want to spiritually put upon their head. The price has been paid. They only have to come and ask of Me, their loving Father. I proved My love by giving One whom I cherished, who was completely righteous, but was willing to become unrighteous so that My many sons and daughters would be made righteous forever by His one sacrifice.

You are only righteous by faith in the One who cleanses and makes you right with Me, My Son, Jesus is His name!

In Your Natal Blood

When I passed by you and saw you rolling about in your blood, I said to you in your blood, "Live"! Yes I said to you still in your natal blood, Live! Ezekiel 16:6

My child on that day you were born, I saw you. Remember I am the One who formed you in your mother's womb. You were fearfully and wonderfully made. I saw you even then as you were rolling around in sin, that sin nature in your members, but I spoke. I prophesied over you my Dear One, my desire, my heart for you. I said to you "Live," while you were still in your natal blood, I spoke life to you. Just as I did to the dead dry bones in Ezekiel's day. I spoke and caused life to come upon those bones.

You are mine. Satan has always spoken death, to kill and destroy the life that I have spoken. Always speak life to your children and to your children's children. Even when they are still in their natal blood prophesy to each child "live" that they would know Me from the beginning through My word. Prophesy that they would grow in understanding and know My Peace, My Love, and My Joy. These will be life to them and health to all their bones. Yes, their bones shall not be dry or dead, but full of life to move about and bring life to others.

My Beloved, as you await the birth of your new grandson put in demonstration My Word to you. I can see you can hardly wait to speak in agreement this word of mine over him. Speak while he is still in his natal blood, the word of life. Life is in the blood. Speak the life of My Blood that cleanses and makes perfect forever that Precious little one's blood and makes him white as snow, though his sins be as scarlet. Yes child, let you and I participate together in agreement and speak forth "Life," telling him to "Live" in the Lord Jesus Christ and My Covenant forever!

This Child is Given to the Lord Forever

27) For this child I prayed, and the Lord has granted my petition made to Him.
28) Therefore, I have given him to the Lord; as long as he lives he is given to the Lord. I Samuel 1:27 & 28

My Chosen One, you remember the day I put this in your heart, all the years you had read this as Hannah's prayer, but not on this day. This day I took it straight to your heart. It was to be yours forever. You know I make each child, son or daughter one at a time. Each with special needs. You saw this not only as a prayer of petition for a newborn baby, but as a prayer for a child, no matter what the age. You, because of my covenant with you, can let your petition be made known and come boldly to me, to My throne of Grace to ask whatever desire you have and it shall be granted according to My Word and Promises.

You remember when My disciples were fishing and I called to them, "Boys (Children) have you caught anything"? These were grown men, but they were still My Beloved children. That is how you feel over your two sons. They may be grown men, but in your heart they will always be your children whom you love, no matter what. Nothing they could ever say or do could ever separate the love you have for these two "Boys"!

My Beloved, as you are my House of Prayer, standing there in My Covenant, abiding in My Word, I will grant the request you ask over your children. There is nothing impossible with Me. I must honor My word. I must grant your petition. After all the desire of your heart was my idea. It was I who thought of My Covenant and My Promises toward you. All I ask is that you ask of Me and I will move Heaven and Earth and see that your petition is granted.

You can now wholly give to Me, in full absolute trust that child whom I love more than you ever have or ever could. After all, that is why I sent My Only Son, the One whom I love, to die, that the utmost petition of your heart for your two sons might now live, and live they will, forever and ever.

Yes, the petition has been granted!

He is Able to Keep

For I know whom I have believed and am fully persuaded that He is able to keep that which I have committed unto Him against that day.   II Timothy 1:12 KJV

Dear One, you remember how this word came alive in your heart; how you had sung this hymn in the Church for years, but up until a certain day, it had only been nice words, a pretty song! There you were with the house all loaded up, moving for the first time away from where you grew up, from all that you knew to a land you knew not, from a South Georgia town to Kansas! You, your husband and two little boys, did not know if you would ever return to the land you had always known, where family and friends were. Oh, how I knew just the word to send, a word fitly spoken to bring peace and encouragement to your heart.

The morning of your departure you sat in a chair alone. Remember, you were going to read this word to me, and out of your heart people and situations you wanted to commit and entrust to Me. Little did you know how my presence was about to speak. Do you remember what I did as you began speaking my word back to Me? I closed your mouth and called, "Linda, Linda, all the desires of your heart have been given, I truly am directing your steps." Then as you were about to respond to Me, I spoke and told you that you could trust Me. I am faithful to do what I say. You left South Georgia with confidence that your God who knows you and knows all, had spoken to you. You thought, "I can't believe God, the Creator of all the universe, sees me and calls me by name. He actually knows *me!*"

I knew all the fears you still had to overcome. After that encounter, you thought you would never doubt or fear again, but as the days passed, you had to fight to believe My Word to you. The Holy Spirit would bring to your remembrance what I said years ago. I reminded you that the desires of your heart are My desires that I placed in your heart.

These desires, especially for your children, are not those natural momentary desires you think out of your mind. They would be earthly and nice for them for the moment. Your desires that are eternal, with an eternal weight of glory shall never be taken away from them. You prayed that they would know Me, love Me, walk in My truth, hear My voice and know My Covenant of Love for them. Yes, those are the desires I am talking about. All else is wood, hay and stubble. At the end of Paul's life, why had this word which had been a small seed planted in his heart become reality? Because over and over in his experiences in life, the only way he could know My keeping power was to give Me something to keep, and then looking back through it all, and be able to say, "Lord, you really were there. I wondered if you really saw, if you really were being faithful to work in that situation." But like Paul, your house of faith is built on a rock that cannot be shaken or moved, it is being built brick upon brick, line upon line, precept upon precept, here a little, there a little. I have spoken, "Heaven and earth shall pass away, but my word is forever settled in heaven." Paul knew this, that is why he could say at the end of his life, "I know whom I have believed and I am fully persuaded (not partially, not half-heartedly but fully confident in my God) that He is able to keep that which I have committed into His keeping. He will keep it until on that day, the day I see Him and all whom I have entrusted to Him who are with Him."

My Word is like a tiny grain of mustard seed. You hear and it is planted in your heart. As I have said, as it is watered through the years it grows into a large tree with many branches and deep roots. I will not only give *you* rest, but I will comfort others that you share with. They can nestle in and one day be able to say with you, "I too am now fully persuaded."

Her Household is Doubly Clothed in Scarlet

She fears not the snow for her family, for all her household are doubly clothed in scarlet. Proverbs 31:21

My Dear Precious One, I have not given you a spirit of fear, My Spirit brings you peace. The Scarlet Cord that runs through the pages of this book, My New Covenant with you, covers and clothes you with righteousness, joy, and peace in my promises to you. There is *life* in the Blood. When the righteous Word that is clean and whiter than snow falls on the sin or the life of those of your family, it will never fall to bring fear, guilt or condemnation to that Dear One. My word only brings conviction, My love, and My life because they are doubly clothed in that Scarlet Blood. The blood assures you that though their sins be as scarlet they shall be white as snow.

That is exactly what My New Covenant does with all your household. Yes, I did not say one or a few, but *all* your household, all those you hold in your heart, trusting me for the very promise. It is not their actions or imperfections you are to look at; look unto Jesus. Look unto the Blood, the Scarlet Blood He shed. You need not fret or be anxious when My word falls on their life because of your heart of faith. You have spent time with me. As I have taken that filthy robe of self righteousness off of you and put on My Robe of Righteousness, I have also put into your heart the faith to clothe your household.

Their bodies belong to Me, inside and out. Yes, their inner selves, clothed by My Spirit and My Word in their heart, and the outer garment that keeps and clothes their natural mind and body, shall be kept. I am maker of it all. They have double protection when my Word of Righteousness and Judgement falls on all your household. For you see, they are doubly clothed!

His Mother Made Him a Robe

Moreover, His mother made him a little robe and brought it to him from year to year when she came up with her husband to offer the yearly sacrifice. I Samuel 2:19

Oh Beloved, remember when I spoke to your heart and told you that the prayer Hannah prayed many years ago could be your prayer for each of your children? It first started with a request, a petition, a desire for a child. That petition we have talked about earlier was granted just as Hannah had prayed. You can also know the petition has been granted to you, so you can safely entrust your child to Me forever! You must declare once and for all, the child is mine; after all, you know I love your child more than you ever have or could. Under My Blood Covenant you must believe and trust me.

In your heart and mind, as your child grows, I want you to come up higher and learn My ways, My thoughts, My desires, My plans. From year to year you must sacrifice your desires, your plans, your fear and control to Me, by faith. My plans are higher than yours. You are spiritually dressing and covering the child you have given Me with My Robe of Righteousness for whatever situation, My Robe is sufficient. Your child is covered and clothed in My Covenant. I honor it and you can rest assured that your child is a marked child to Me forever.

You know how when you go to a school function and all the children, yours and other people's children, are in a play or in a sporting event, you watch for only one—the "apple of your eye". Only one number on the jersey stands out to you. If a player is hurt, you listen for one number and one number only. Well, I look for the Robe; I look to see how faithful you are to cover and dress your child with forgiveness, love, peace, joy and righteousness. Do you see your child in the authority I have given to that Precious One, the power and position as one seated in heavenly places with Me? Yes, as you abide in My promises and My will for your child, you are dressing that anointed one in my Robe. Your child will grow in beauty from year-to-year even unto maturity in the latter years. I honor that Robe, My Robe. Be faithful to see your child covered in it, no matter how filthy the skin (the flesh)!

No Words Shall Fall to the Ground

Samuel grew; the Lord was with him and let none of his words fall to the ground. I Samuel 3:19

    As I promised Hannah I also promise you, My Beloved. Yes, because her petition was granted, she could trust me, the One who created her precious little one, "the apple of her eye." She committed her child to me, the one whom she loved more than life itself. I take charge, because I am Love and all wise. I am the One who says if you, being evil love your children, how much more I love them with My perfect pure love. Because you are trusting Me I watch over your child, carefully watching the seed of My Word being planted in a heart. Then I watch the growth of that Word from a little sprout, a small sapling into a full grown kernel of wheat. Yes, as your child grows, if you give your child to Me, I will be with him or her as they grow. As I am with them, I promised that My Words which I have put within you shall not depart out of their mouth or out of their children's mouth. My words that they speak shall not go forth in vain, shall not fall to the ground and die, but shall be alive, sharper than any two-edged sword, accomplishing all that it is sent forth to do. If you look at what I say, be secure. It is I who is in charge and I let none of their words (My Words) fall. Remember when I called to Samuel, he being a little lad did not recognize my voice, but as he grew My voice became very clear to him. As the ears of his heart matured and he spoke as he heard a familiar voice that he recognized as a family member, Samuel spoke, "thus saith the Lord." He recognized a father who desired to speak to his children and have his children speak back to him. Hannah, a mother who loved her child so much, knew I would give her security in her heart, to trust Me in all the plans for good and not for evil for this child's life. You know yourself, now that your children are grown, how I show glimpses of My faithfulness.

Remember the day your oldest son Trevor called and said, "Mama, I have been reading the book of Psalms and I just realized those songs we sang as I was growing up, are from this book." He began singing them to you over the phone. Nothing could have sounded better to your ears than that! A few weeks later Todd, your youngest son called and asked about those same songs! He wanted to teach them to his wife, Cindy, so the two of them could teach them to their son.

What were just songs have now become My Words to them. They are hearing My Word, hearing My Voice.

None shall fall to the ground!

You and Your Descendants

Behold, I establish My covenant or pledge with you and with your descendants after you...Genesis 9:9

I want you to behold, to look at in awe and wonderment at what My Covenant holds! Stop and look and listen to my wonderful promise to you and your descendants after you. My covenant or pledge is with you. I establish all of it. My covenant is so broad and encompassed so much it will take all eternity to enlarge your heart to take it all in. My Covenant is to provide everything a soul needs to be made in my likeness; to walk in my ways, to be delivered and made whole, to be a full grown matured son or daughter, to know me as an Everlasting Father, to know My Son Jesus and to be as a bride filled and walking in My Love. If you notice, it is *My covenant*, I wrote it all out from the beginning. My pledge to you cost me my very heart, My Only Son. I was required to give him up, sow Him into the earth, that by your beholding what I have promised to you through Him, would bring Me many sons and daughters.

He was the payment for all My Covenant to you and not only to you, but my promise to you concerning your descendants. If this so great sacrifice was made because of my great love, all I ask of you dear child is that you believe me for all the promises I have made in your heart to you! Even after you are with me My

Covenant cannot and will not fail. I will establish all of it with your descendants. I'll not lose one of them, whomsoever you commit to me until on that day. You can be fully persuaded I am able and will keep! I am not One that will lie to you. Yes, on that day in the beginning when I counted the cost of My Covenant I said, "Yes." You were worth it, and I have been saying "Yes" to you ever since, because of Jesus, who paid the price so that all My Promises can be Yes and So Be It!

You and Your Family Shall Come into the Ark

12) And God looked upon the world and saw how degenerate, debased, and vicious it was, for all humanity had corrupted their way upon the earth and lost their true direction.
18) But I will establish my covenant (promise, pledge) with you, and you shall come into the ark – you, and your sons and your wife and your sons' wives with you. Genesis 6:12,18

Oh, how I am still looking upon My World, the people whom I have created, who were fearfully and wonderfully made as spoken in Psalm 139. This is still true with births every day. I am still after My creation to have and bring many sons and daughters into My family. Beloved, I am looking at this day and weeping with a father's and a mother's heart as I see how all of humanity has corrupted it's way upon the earth and has lost its true direction. It breaks My heart to see how each has to suffer the consequences of going on his own way. It is still the same Beloved, there is nothing new under the sun. The three ways that lead to this are still the lust of the eyes, lust of the flesh, and the pride of life. As you see yourself and your children at times lose their true direction, what an opportunity to stand in the gap for them and spiritually build that ark, My covenant in your heart concerning them. What a joy! What a promise I have given you!

I have made a pledge with you. Once again I have made a way.

It is a promise to one person who will dare to receive and believe Me for such a wonderful Covenant. My Covenant is with you concerning your whole household. I said, as I establish My Covenant (in your heart and in your mouth) you shall come into that Covenant not only you, but it is a promise to you for all your house. By faith they are in the ark.

Oh, Dear One, it is all by trust and faith in My Word to you. Do not say, "yes, but what if" with many reasons. Did I not say have the faith of a little child who always asks not "how" but "when"? Only that kind of faith can receive a promise like this.

Yes, as this world comes into gross darkness and becomes more degenerate, my people will be safe in this Ark of My Covenant. The working of my hands includes their whole house because of the heart of faith of one. They will look forward to the Blessed Hope of My Coming.

Stones of Remembrance

3) Take twelve stones out of the midst of the Jordan from the place where the priest's feet stood firm; carry them over with you and leave them at the place where you lodge tonight.
6) That this may be a sign among you when your children ask in time to come, what do these stones mean to you?
7) Then you shall tell them that the waters of the Jordan were cut off before the ark of the covenant of the Lord; when it passed over the Jordan, the waters of the Jordan were cut off. So these stones shall be to the Israelites a memorial forever. Joshua 4: 3,6,7

    Do you remember how this story in Joshua literally became your story? You took your bag of apples, chickens, lambs and fish to share at a meeting in Toccoa, Georgia many years ago. After you had spoken, your dear friend Jayne spoke out from the back of the room and said, "Linda, you have shared your Stones of Remembrance as they did in the book of Joshua." After that day you pondered all the Stones of Remembrance in your heart and home. In a special way you related to My Words in Joshua of long ago. When I take you out of the world's way of thinking, you can see and know My acts in a moment. Remember it is a walk and a lifetime of learning My Ways through which you really get to know Me. My Ways are higher. That is why I have said over and over, "Trust in the Lord with all your heart and lean not on your own understanding." In the midst of every situation of life I am there with you, delivering you, teaching you, growing you in Me. Nothing is lost. Not only will I never leave you or forsake you, but I will never even relax my hold on you. When in life the situation (like the waters at Jordan at flood time) seems to overwhelm you, in the midst of the very situation you are in, I will give you My Word. It will bring peace and rest to your very soul, your mind and emotions, so that you can stand firm in My Word. This is My promise to you in that situation. When your children ask you, "What do these apples, chickens, lambs and fish that are around our house mean to you?", you can share that moment in time when I showed you in My Word how I dried up the overwhelming waters of life. Out of it, you have a special Stone of Remembrance that will be a memorial, a story forever of My love and My faithfulness. My Covenant, My Ark of the Covenant shall pass through all the drowning waters of your life. My promise to you concerning you and your household shall always be remembered to those with whom you share. My promise shall bless and encourage them to see that they have their own stones, so that their children may ask, "What do these stones mean to you?"

You Shall Let Your Children Know

22) You shall let your children know, Israel came over this Jordan on dry ground.
23) For the Lord your God dried up the waters of the Jordan for you until you passed over, as the Lord Your God did to the Red Sea, which He dried up for us until we passed over.
24) That all the peoples of the earth may know that the hand of the Lord is mighty and that you may reverence and fear the Lord your God forever. Joshua 4: 22,23,24

You shall let your children know you came through this situation on dry ground! Your Father God never relaxed His hold on you. He gave a Word to you so you did not get overwhelmed or succumb to that pressure of life, but trusted Him who knows best. He would not let you down or forsake you; He was walking you through His ways, drying up the waters in your mind and walking you to completely dry ground.

My daughter, did you see where I said I dried up the waters so you would not get caught in the middle of the situation? I intend for you to pass over to the other side. I never intended for you to lodge or camp out in all the fear, anger or doubt of your mind. As I walk with you and send My Word, you stand firm in my word and trust me. I dry up the overwhelming waters until you pass over.

Well, Dear One, every time you share a "Stone of Remembrance" you are looking back at flood time in your life, where life was overwhelming to your heart. I brought My word which dried up the waters in that situation to cause you to stand firm in My Covenant of Promise to you. I took you over to the other side and each time you looked back, you gathered all those stones that made your house strong within you. The chief cornerstone is Jesus Christ who holds it all together. His shed blood calms the waters and dries them up because He makes the Covenant alive. So be it. You and your household are passing to the other side on dry ground. Because these stones are so real and alive, when you speak of them, you are reverencing Me . . . the Lord your God forever!

The Stone as a Pillow Under Your Head

11) And he came to a certain place and stayed there overnight because the sun was set. Taking One of the stones of the place, he put it under his head and lay down there to sleep.
12) And he dreamed that there was a ladder set up on the Earth and the top of it reached to heaven and the angels of God were ascending and descending on it!
13) And behold, the Lord stood over and beside him and said, "I am the Lord, the God of Abraham your Father [Forefather] and the God of Isaac; I will give to you and to your descendants the Land on which you are lying." Genesis 28:11,12,13

Oh, how I have taught you this one. Even though it is the familiar story of long ago about Jacob's ladder, it is alive. When you come to a certain place, a certain situation in your life, it sometimes seems it is an overnight experience. It will be seemingly dark and the sun will be set. It will be like the midnight hour in life. You won't understand why; you may wonder where I am! But you know now, I want you to know Me, your Father, by learning My ways, not by just knowing My acts. You have learned like Jacob to take one of the stones (My Word to you) out of that place (that situation in life), and put it under your head and lie down to sleep. My Word in the midst of the storm will bring comfort and sleep. Know I am watching over everything that concerns you, My Beloved. You may sleep, but I never slumber nor sleep. I am faithful to you in keeping those of My Covenant.

Yes, there will be those certain times in your life. You may wonder if I hear, if I care, if I am awake. You may take even what I said in this story and make this stone a comforting pillow for your head and go to sleep. When Jacob quit running, and quit wrestling with what I was doing in his life, when he stood still and rested, then he saw Me. He saw his God, his Father, his Redeemer when he rested in that dark time in his life. He saw this ladder (Jacob's Ladder) set up on earth (where Jacob was) and the top of it reached to heaven with my angels going up and down. Upward to Me and downward to you-total communication. In these times, and always as in this story, if your heart's eyes could open and see, this is your ladder. While you rest in me, I let you know I stand over and beside you. I am the Lord, your God, and I will give to you and your descendants the land on which you are lying. For you see you are finding out, Dear One, just as Jacob did, there is an open way between you and me. For you, Jesus is the ladder, He is seated by me. He lives forever to make intercession for you and to make good that stone (My Word that you are resting on). When Jacob, found Me everywhere, just like you found me in your own heart, he found a big stone to fall asleep on. This is relationship. This land you lie on, I will give to you and to your children's children. My Son, Jesus Christ will be their ladder.

Five Smooth Stones

40) then he took his staff in his hand and chose five smooth stones out of the brook and put them in his shepherd's bag and his sling was in his hand and he drew near the Philistine.
49) David put his hand into his bag and took out a stone and slung it, and it struck the Philistine, sinking into his forehead and he fell on his face to the earth
50) David prevailed over the Philistine with a sling and a stone and slew him. But no sword was in David's hand. I Samuel 17:40,49,50

Oh, how David, a man after my own heart, knew who he was, a Covenant man. David knew that the weapons of his warfare are not carnal, but mighty through Me to pulling down strongholds. He knew being in covenant with Me, I would not forsake or fail him. That is why he declared that he was well able to bring down the giant, Goliath, because he (David) had the Covenant. In the New Covenant through the name and blood of my Dear Son Jesus Christ, how much more this situation with David must mean to you today. As the giant in your life tries to defeat you from receiving My pledge to you concerning your household, take the staff of My direction and the authority of the name of Jesus in your hand as David chose five smooth stones. To you that would mean you have received My Covenant for a given situation. My special grace will bring you My Words to bring light, hope, faith and assurance.

The stones came out of the brook. This means through many years, through the washing of the Word, My Covenant is made effective and sure for your situation. As you hide my words in your heart, they become like those smooth stones in David's shepherd bag. So when Satan comes, the father of lies, who has no truth in him, you can pursue him. Draw out my Word for the stone that strikes the head, kills the lie. You don't need a worldly sword, only My Word. David only needed a Word, one stone for that situation in his life. It is written that later on he met up with four other liars, Goliath's brothers. He had four stones left from the five in his shepherd's bag. Oh, Precious One, store up my word in your heart that you too may overcome with one word. One stone from me brings down a lie. Speak the truth of My Covenant.

David's heart, like yours, had been circumcised. Emanuel's blood flows through your veins. You are of Me, and the whole world lies in the power of the evil one. Have no fear, I have overcome the world. Many were spared that day because a young man believed Me and My Covenant. I say to you, believe Me your God and My Covenant, and you and your household shall be saved.

The Scarlet Cord

13) Save alive my Father and Mother, my brothers and sisters and all they have, and deliver us from death.
18) Behold, when we come into the land, you shall bind this scarlet cord in the window through which you let us down, and you shall bring your father and mother, your brothers and all your father's household into your house.
21) And she said according to your words, so it is. Then she sent them away and they departed; and she bound the scarlet cord in the window. Joshua 2:13,18,21

Remember that day you were walking and talking with Me about believing for your whole household? You knew how many of my promises in your heart and mind concerned your children and your children's children. You asked, "Was this household covenant for other members?" Immediately I answered before you called. I said "remember Rahab." Faith in my promise was found in Rahab. I look for faith in My Covenant. Rahab acted on faith. In the world, she was not perfect. She was a known temple prostitute. The day faith came to her, her father, her mother, her brethren, and all her kindred were saved from destruction.

The whole situation in and around you may look like destruction. When I look upon My world I see your flesh has not been perfect. If you will stand in the gap, hide the message of My Covenant in your heart, ask me to save your whole house you are believing for, and hang out the cord that cannot be broken, I will be faithful to the Covenant I have sworn to you. Can't you hear me saying to My ministering angel, "When I send destruction, go to Linda's house, bring her out and all she has, her whole household, all the ones for whom she has been holding out the Red Cord, the Blood of my Precious Son. You must save all of them from the destruction because I swore to her through My Word. I esteem My Word to be above My Name. Heaven and earth may pass away, but My Words to Linda shall never pass away. I will be true to her and bring out all whom she has in her house."

What the blood was to the houses of Israel on the doorposts during the first Passover night in Egypt, the scarlet cord in the window was to the house of Rahab. Her sinful years of ignorance, I forgave! I honored her in direct lineage with My Son, Jesus Christ and had her written in the book of Hebrews as a *Hero of Faith.* She did not know that night all that would be done for her from that one act of obedience and faith.

You and Your House Shall Live

17) The city and all that is in it shall be devoted to the Lord [for destruction]: only Rahab the harlot and all who are with her in her house shall live, because she hid the messengers whom we sent.
22) Joshua said to the two men who had spied out the land, Go into the harlot's house and bring out the woman and all she has, as you swore to her.
23) So the young men, the spies, went in and brought out Rahab, her father, and mother, her brethren, and all that she had; and they brought out all her kindred and set them outside the camp of Israel. Joshua 6:17,22,23

Again the story is told. Today bind (stand firm in My Promises to you) that red scarlet cord out the window of your heart. No matter how small a window that lets a ray of sunshine of the truth of My Word in your heart, it shall be enough for me to act because of the love for My Son and for you. Acknowledge My pain and His, so that you may receive this promise and message of hope to you and to all that are in your house. My Covenant is broad enough to cover you, your children, your children's children, mothers, fathers, sisters, brothers and all your kindred. Keep that red cord hung out, I will deliver and do all that I have sworn to you.

What a natural mess Rahab the harlot and her household were

in! Total heathen disarray had been present for years. I was looking for one heart in one household in Jericho that said, "Yes" to My Covenant. I am still looking for My covenant in each heart, my agreement that I swear to you because of the price that was paid by my Precious Son, Jesus Christ. Please, like Rahab, hide the message in your heart. I am looking over the whole earth to see my *red cord* and show myself strong on your behalf. I look for faith in My Covenant. As you let the *red cord* down, I promise, I promise, I will not let you down!

God Remembered His Covenant

16) But while he lingered, the man seized him and his wife and his two daughters by the hand, for the Lord was merciful to him; and they brought him forth and set him outside the city and left him there.
22) Make haste and take refuge there, for I cannot do anything until you arrive there.
29) When God ravaged and destroyed the cities of the plain, He [earnestly] remembered Abraham [imprinted and fixed him indelibly on His mind] and He sent Lot out of the midst of the overthrow when He overthrew the cities where Lot lived. Genesis 19:16,22,29

What a picture to you of My Covenant over your household! Here was Lot and his family living in Sodom and Gomorrah, a heathen land. He was the nephew and extended family to Abraham. Because I had made my blood covenant real and available to Abraham and because of his faith in My pledge to him concerning his household, when it got bad in Sodom and Gomorrah, I had to warn my servant Abraham it would be destroyed. I could not destroy a place until I had been faithful to Abraham, because he believed Me for that agreement to deliver his family from destruction.

How much more will I show my faithfulness to you, your own immediate household, your children and your children's children.

Even while they may be in a distant place, spiritually or physically, even while they linger or hang around, I will send strong angels to seize them by the hand, remove them, and bring them out. I must be faithful to you. You are under the better covenant. I see the Precious blood of My Dear Son, Jesus Christ, covering you and your household. Because of My Covenant, my angels who were sent to destroy Sodom and Gomorrah, told Lot they could not raise a hand or do anything until they got him and his family out of there. And the Word says while Lot and his family were lingering, slow about what to do, God ordered those ministering Angels, to his heirs of salvation, to seize them by the hand and get them out of there. God was faithful only because He remembered Abraham and His covenant with Him, not because of a covenant with Lot. Lot and his family benefited because of God's Covenant with one man, Abraham.

Now I look for My Covenant. All it takes is your faith; I will not forget you or your family when destruction comes. I will gather you and your family to Me. I can do nothing until all arrive safely in that place, the place I have called you to be with Me.

That is My Covenant—My Covenant is in Jesus' shed blood that is forever pouring over you and your household.

Your Children Shall Return

15) Thus says the Lord, A voice is heard in Ramah, lamentation and bitter weeping. Rachael is weeping for her children; she refuses to be comforted for her children because they are no more.
16) Thus says the Lord: Restrain your voice from weeping and your eyes from tears, for your work shall be rewarded, says the Lord; and [your children] shall return from the enemy's land.
17) And there is hope for your future, says the Lord; your children shall come back to their own country. Jeremiah 31:15,16,17

Oh, how I hear the cry of My children, especially a mother's prayer and request for her children. My promises are true and faithful. My ear is not deaf that it cannot hear your cry, nor is my arm shortened that it cannot reach out in response to your cry. I will reach with My outstretched arm anywhere it needs to go to bring that child back to where he or she belongs. When you look only at the circumstances, your children seem to be no more living in the land. They seem not to be possessing that which I desire for them. They have gone astray out of the land. Do not just sit there with no comfort, no hope. I have told you to have hope with joy and expectation because of what I tell you in My Word. Restrain yourself; keep from crying anymore. You do not need to voice this situation with your child or children anymore. Why not? I will reward your work: Your prayer requests in my Son's

Name, your faith in trusting Me to do what I said I would do, your hanging out the red cord through the window of you heart. I call it work, not the working of your own hands, but a work that is a labor to enter that rest. That rest says, cease from your own labor in this and rest in the fact that I will bring them back from the enemy's land. That is why there is hope for your future. I said, "Your children shall come back to their own country." A country or city not made with men's hands, but whose builder and maker is Father God.

I Will Hiss for Your Children

8) I will hiss for them [as the keeper does for his bees] and gather them in, for I have redeemed them and they shall increase as they have increased before.
9) And though I sow them among nations, yet they shall [earnestly] remember me in far countries and with their children they shall live and shall return [to God and the Land He gave them].
10) I will bring them home again from the Land of Egypt and gather them out of Assyria, and I will bring them into the land, and room enough shall not be found for them. Zechariah 10:8,9,10

Here it is again—My Covenant! As I earnestly remember My pledge to you, see what I do. Though I sow your children out in the world, I am their keeper. I have told you I will not fail you or forsake you. I will gather them in just like a mother hen gathers in her chicks. The reason I gather them in is because I promised you I have redeemed them. They are mine. I have called them by name.

How many times when your own sons, Trevor and Todd, would come home during their high school years and tell you how a flash of remembrance of Me would come to them in a situation. On one Halloween night, they went with other boys and girls to the front steps of the town spook house with the fortune teller.

As your two sons stood there, I brought to their remembrance that I am the Lord, their God, who guides and the only one who speaks and directs their paths. Without a moments hesitation they said, "Let's get out of here." I hissed for them that night, on that front porch. My two covenant boys, covered in the blood of My Dear Son, had no business seeking guidance from a tool of Satan to put their minds and lives under that fear and bondage. This is just one of many instances I acted on behalf of My Covenant.

You notice how many times I said, "I gather." I shall bring them home again, not only shall they live in the land, but also their children. This is once again why I say I give My Beloved sleep and desire for you to enter My rest. I neither slumber nor sleep but am watching over My Covenant, to do what I have sworn to you. I am the Doer. You are the believer!

Jesus Prayer for Your Children

John 17:15
Father,
15) I do not ask that You will take them out of the world, but that You will keep and protect them from the evil one.

Oh, what a prayer, my own heart being poured out of My Son's heart for the many sons and daughters that would come after. My Son Jesus counted the cost and declared before Me and the whole world that you are worth the price. My Son asked that I would not take you or your children out of the world, but that in the midst of it I would keep and protect you and your household. He asked that you and your children be sanctified and made holy through the price of His work on the cross, His shedding of His blood and that you might become one in Him and My very heart. The heart of God, that three stranded cord, (they in me and I in them) cannot be broken, My Blood Covenant. He asked that you and your household become perfectly united in My truth and know how much I love Jesus. Jesus, My Son because of His very soul that was poured forth, asked that I keep by my side the ones that I would entrust to His keeping. I pour out my love to them that was for them before the foundation of the earth. Jesus, My Son asked that I would make known to you and your children My Name. I am the one who made them and who made Heaven and earth. I will reveal My character and Myself to them that I would continue to be made known in their lives. Above all Jesus asked that the love that I had bestowed upon Him may be in you and in your children, that He may be in them.

Well, My Beloved, what more can I say? My Son Jesus, who counted the cost, paid the price that He could say, "It is finished." There is no more to pay. Just receive the promise of this covenant. It is yours; yours and those who would come after you. Like I said My Words and My Very Heart were in that prayer with the Holy Spirit empowering it. This prayer was from Me. It was My idea. I say yes, yes to this prayer. I desire that you say yes. For in My Son, His prayers have been answered. In Him all the promises are "Yes" and "So Be It." This is My Covenant!

In the Father's Hand

29) My Father, Who has given them to Me is greater and mightier than all [else]; and no one is able to snatch [them] out of the Father's hand.
30) I and the Father are One! John 10:29,30

Oh, what a promise to you! My Father who made heaven and earth, who fashioned all new life, who is greater and mightier than all else, has you and your children in the palm of His powerful hand. I told you earlier, I earnestly remember you are indelibly written on the palm of My hand. I remember My Covenant with those I have bound Myself to in My great love for you.

Please trust Me when I tell you no one is able to snatch your children out of My Father's hand. Did I not tell you even a little sparrow does not ever fall to the ground without My Father knowing about it? What I desire for you to see is that I and My Father are one! We are one in our desires, one in power, one in our will for you and your loved ones. Become, one with us Dear One. I in Him, He in Me and you in us. Your desires are our desires. Those intangible desires that are not of this world. They are for those who will be for all eternity in the palm of My hand.

I Will Not Lose One of Them

37) <u>Those (Your Children)</u> , Whom My Father gives (entrusts) to Me will come to Me; and <u>they</u> Who come to Me I will most certainly not cast out (I will never, no never), reject Who comes to Me.
39) This is the will of Him Who sent me, that I should not lose <u>one</u> Who He has given me, but that I should give new life and raise <u>them</u> up at the last day. John 6:37,39

You ask can this really be so? It is so wonderful. It brings such joy, such peace to know this in your heart. I want you to put your child's name in the blanks. Yes, call him or her by name and speak, receive and believe this word of promise over them. I pledge this in My Covenant to you. I promise that child you ask me for and you give to Me will come to Me; that is the first promise to you. After that child comes to Me, I tell you most certainly My second promise is that I will never, no never reject that child you and I call by name. My third promise to you is the will of My Father God that I should not lose that child, whom He has given Me, but that I should give new life to that child and raise them up on that last day.

Dare to believe this, I know you say to Me out of your mind and reasoning, "yes, but," I see my child's flesh and all his imperfect ways. Did I not tell you in My Word, "Do not look or consider the flesh, but look and only consider Me, the High Priest of your confession. You can come boldly to me, that throne of grace, and make your request known. I said *Yes* to whatever you asked according to My promise to you, My will. Trust in My Words, not the flesh."

I will raise them up on the last day!

Your Confidence is in Me

14) This is the confidence which we have in Him: [we are sure] that if we ask anything according to His will, He listens to and hears us.
15) And if (since) we [positively] know that He listens to us in whatever we ask, we also know that we have [as a present possession] the requests made of Him. I John 5:14,15

Oh Beloved One, I want you to have confidence in Me, your Father, when you read the petition of My Dear Son that all the requests of my children could be *yes*. He asked that I would keep all the ones He committed into My keeping, and not lose one, that I would save and keep each one from the evil one in the world. He asked that I would give you as a present possession the request you have made according to my will. Remember how I told you in My word, when you speak forth My Covenant I listen to you and write down the very words you speak and put them in My book of remembrance with your name on it? You will ask Me, "Father when did I say this?" You may forget, but I will not. I will have the pleasure of bringing it back to your remembrance. In fact, have I not told you I have put every tear of yours in a special bottle? Not one drop of your sorrow in life has gone unnoticed by Me. Did I not tell you I am touched by your feelings? When I speak of the silence in heaven, when at that moment in time the incense of your prayers are poured forth, that is when you prayed according to my will and I hushed all of heaven and hearkened to your words and answered, "*yes*, the request is yours." You can be confident. Your confidence is in Me. I will do it on that day, the day of the Lord. You will not be disappointed for what you were trusting Me.

Bringing Forth Children Blessed of the Lord

23) They shall not labor in vain or bring forth [children] for sudden terror or calamity; for they shall be the descendants of the blessed of the Lord, and their offspring with them. Isaiah 65:23

As you labor to enter My rest, to rest in all I have promised in My Covenant to you concerning your children and their offspring, do not even entertain the idea that I am a Father who will answer you with terror or calamity for your children. For they are My descendants and will be forever blessed by Me. You know how grieved I was when I brought my children out of Egypt, because they leaned to their own understanding of Me as their Father. All they wanted of Me were My acts. They wanted Me to act immediately on their behalf to make them comfortable in life and in their flesh. Remember I told them, "You know My acts but you do not know My ways." I told them then as I am telling you now, Dear One, My ways are past finding out. My ways are higher than your ways. I have said to you, "Trust Me in all your ways, commit to me and I will bring it to pass. The *trial* of your faith, not your faith, is what is more Precious than gold to Me."

I told my children in Egypt I was bringing forth a trial of their faith to bring forth gold and to do them good in the end. There

85

were those precious little covenanted ones whom I told to dress in silver and gold. They were dressed from the beginning, redeemed with the fullness of me, yet when the trial of their faith came, they complained I had brought their children out of Egypt (the world) to let them die in the desert. They spoke not what I had promised to them. I knew in the beginning what they were going to do. That is why I told them to dress their children in silver and gold. I said, "because of unbelief you have spoken evil of Me and you will not and cannot possess My promises without trusting Me."

Your children are going into My promised land. They shall possess the good of the land, not to die in it, but to live out their experiences of life. They shall possess My promise in the land and declare, I am a Father filled with Love and Goodness to them.

I Will Save Your Children

I will contend with those who contend with you, and your children I will save. Isaiah 49:25 NIV

    I hope by now you are seeing I watch over My Word and I am continually acting and moving in the earth concerning My Word to you to perform it. When you take the death of My Precious Dearly Beloved Son, Jesus, as seriously and as real as I do, My Covenant to you can never be in vain. Know that because of your faith in me, I will contend with the evil one who contends with you-the one who has been a liar from the beginning, the father of lies. No truth can be found in him. My Son is truth. He is called Faithful and True.

    On that day you will declare, Father You have been Faithful and True to me concerning your Covenant over me and my children. Jesus is the One that contended with Satan and won! When the mirage of lies come like a flood to your mind to cause you in any way to discount My promises of truth to you, I will contend and My Word will raise up a standard against your enemy. I will give safety. Let them know they are safe forever in My everlasting arms in whatever situation life has brought them. I will ease, and comfort them with "My love," "My peace" and "My joy." Just trust Me, I will, I will do it. I cannot lie.

The Apple of My Eye

10) He found him in a desert land, in the howling void of the wilderness; He kept circling around him, He scanned him [penetratingly]. He kept him as the apple of His eye.
11) As an eagle that stirs up her nest, that flutters over her young, He spread abroad His wings and He took them, He bore them on His pinions. Deuteronomy 32:10-11

You did not find Me, I found you. I swore to you I will go out and find your children and your children's children. My finding and My blessing is from generation to generation because of My Covenant with you. Remember Mephibosheth, years after Jonathan was dead and gone? The Covenant was still alive in heaven and earth that David made with Jonathan to bless his household. It was asked, "Is there anyone in the house of Jonathan that I may go find and show my kindness to?" How much more will I do that for you Beloved. That is where I found you, all my children are in a howling void waste place. My promise to you is that I will find each of your children in whatever desert land they might be in. When I find them, I will keep circling them with My single eye and I will keep them as the "Apple of My Eye." Each of them will know how I call them by name, I know them, they are mine. I sought after them and they will always have a very special place in my heart. I love each one of them with My everlasting love. The love thereby I drew them was not with a rod, but with my loving kindness. My goodness, not wrath, will lead them to repentance.

Each child being the "Apple of My Eye" means every detail of their life concerns Me. I am watching over every concern, every thought. They are my sons and daughters. I have plans for them, plans for good and not for evil, to give each of them a future and a hope. I will bring them into the fullness of this hope and plan of who they are. I give the picture of the mother eagle and her young. In my word the scripture begins as a she, a mother eagle. She stirs up her nest, she flutters over her young. I stir up the nest. Out of my love and plans for your children, I remove those comfortable downy feathers by causing situations that are sometimes painful and uncomfortable to stir up the nest. A mother's heart wants to continue to fluff up the nest and flutter over her young. A father's heart seeks to push his children into a complete relinquishment to me. It will seem scary at first. You will ask, "Oh, what if they hit the ground?" Look who is there with the everlasting arms to catch them before they hit the ground. The great I Am is there. Oh, you just trust my arms. Your arms and wings are not wide enough or powerful enough. Watch Me! I am the great I Am. I Am the Great Mother and Father Eagle! I spread abroad My wings to carry you and your children, however broad those wings need to be.

I the Lord your God will bear you and them on my pinions, I will carry you and your household forever and ever.

I Want to be Mother Hen

... How often I have desired and yearned to gather your children together around Me, as a hen gathers her young under her wings but you would not! Luke 13:34

Oh Dear One, how I wanted to get this picture across to you; how I desire to write it again and again on your heart. This is how you begin to enter My rest. See who I really am, who I am in your life, and what I want to be not only to you, but to your children. Oh, how I desire and yearn to gather your children together around Me, as a hen gathers her young under her wings; but you would not!

Beloved, remember how many years ago the words on this page became alive to you and were planted in your heart. My Word, that is sharper than any two-edged sword, began cutting away fear and replaced it with peace.

Yes, as you tell your story you will bring My Peace to many a mother's heart, especially during the dark midnight hour. This word is like Jacob's Stone that he used as a pillow for his head, to sleep and rest on. This word will help you find comfort to know all is well. Yes, I want you to comfort My people as I bring this wonderful Stone of Remembrance to your mind and heart.

When your son Trevor was about to turn sixteen you had the fear that comes to every mother's heart. Becoming sixteen means independence with a driver's license. Up until then you had been in control somewhat, but now you had to let go. Now your mind might let all those imaginations take over, especially if there is a flat tire, and he is not home within ear or eye gate. You remember well that tormenting week, the fear and thoughts that were raging in your mind. Your emotions were like the waters at flood-tide at the River Jordan. As I literally quieted and hushed the waters for them, I did for you. I sent My Word and you received a Stone of Remembrance out of that situation that would be for many days to come.

As that D-Day (Driver's Day) approached, You opened My Book and there you saw it. It was not as you had seen it before with little or no meaning. It had always read O Jerusalem, Jerusalem, but this time you heard me call you by name, O Linda, Linda. You had heard me call you years earlier when I called you by name twice. I gave you My Word, "For I know whom I have believed and I am fully persuaded that He is able to keep that which I have committed unto Him until that day." You saw how personal I am to call you by name. The emphasis of twice shows how much I yearn to get My Word across to you. I wanted to show you that it is the mother, not the children, that would not let Me be Mother Hen. I wanted to be Mother Hen to your children if you would let Me. What joy and peace began to spring forth that day. As the Comforter promised to come in situations like this, I came. As your son turned sixteen that day, the fear was not all gone but was greatly buffeted as he drove out the driveway and honked the horn and smiled. You had a choice that day to abide in fear, which I do not give, or to abide in Me. "Linda, Linda, I want to be Mother Hen, will you let Me?"

That was many years ago. Time has proven and is still proving and will prove again and again, I AM THE GREAT MOTHER HEN!

Long after those teen--age years--years of seeing My Faithfulness as Mother Hen over your children--the phone rang. Your son, Trevor, not a teen-ager now but a grown man in his thirties, called to say he had been to a Men's business luncheon in downtown Atlanta at the Holiday Inn. It so happened a man he just met sitting next to him at the table was a lawyer who also had a prison ministry. The man told Trevor, "I want you to read a poem one of the inmates wrote and gave me last week." Trevor read the poem and immediately thought of all those years of growing up seeing those stuffed chickens all over the house, under the Mother Hen's wings. Always knowing, he was one of those chickens. He knew **I had spoken** once again to his heart of My Covenant over him.

The Poem

Lord—knowing some of what I am supposed to do
Keeping on that course first, last and always to serve you
I did so bad, on so many choices
When all I really wanted was loving voices
Events in my life kept that away, away
Sometimes, golden moments would come day by day
Everlasting love in this mortal life I can't find
So Lord, please, please won't you be always in my mind
So bind me Lord to your will and way
For I know now, that's where I want and should stay
I'll be a little baby chick and you be

                Mother Hen
                Mother Hen
                Mother Hen

And every day I say thank you, thank you,
                Amen
                Amen
                Amen

                Author Unknown

I Desire to Gather Your Children Around Me

~ 🍎 ~

How often would I have gathered your children together as a mother hen gathers her brood under her wings, and you <u>refused!</u> Matthew 23: 37

My children always have thought of me as a He, the Father which I am. I also have the heart of every mother. As for the children, did I not say a mother may forget her suckling baby, but oh, how I would never ever forget! You remember I am El Shaddai, which means *"many breasted One."* I am the Mother who has all the nourishment needed to provide an endless supply of whatever is needed to that Precious One held close to my breast. Please do not ever accuse me of not having the love of a mother, the tender, caring love that would die for her own. Why do you think I put a mother's love in my children in the first place?

How well I understand the heart of a mother. I have written two times, not once, but twice describing Myself as one having the love of a mother. Earlier I gave you the picture of a mother eagle. Now I say "Look at the Mother Hen." Look how she gathers her little chicks under her wings when she sees a black storm brewing, ever attentive to where those little chicks are. All your life you have heard the expression, "madder than an old wet setting hen." You do not want to get near a brood of chicks with the mother hen near. In times of danger, she is near!

So, Dearly Beloved, I chose in My Word to look at the mother hen, to show how I want to be to your children; but you refused to let me! Commit your children to Me. This picture of a mother hen shows My protection, as El Shaddai, My love is far greater.

Years ago I showed you in My Word that I wanted to be like a Mother Hen over your children if you would let Me. A knock came at your door. A friend you had not seen in over a year, Agnes, had heard you were moving and had brought a gift to you. Agnes was creative with her handiwork. Well, there she stood with a stuffed mother hen and three chicks. She had no idea of the message I had placed in your heart just a few days before. You shared it all with your friend that day. You could not figure out why there were three chicks. You only had two sons, could the third one be for Charlie? You knew how easy it is for wives to be like mother hens in their household even over their husbands. I wanted you to learn to commit your children and your husband to Me. I am the Mother Hen when you let Me!

Those chickens snuggle next to the stuffed mother hen on your shelf in the sitting room, so that every person who walks in that room may see. If only they could see the depth of My promise behind that stuffed grouping.

Oh, what a comforter I am. I am the Great Comforter! My Covenant was real to you when your daddy died. Death can seem like a dark midnight hour experience but in the midst I sent My Word to bring light and hope. My Precious One, how you needed that light and hope that was within you to be sparked through that time. During those few days before the funeral, you visited a store and there was the picture of a young girl pushing a group of young baby chicks over to the mother hen. You bought that picture because it reminded you of My Word to you years earlier. I wanted to be "Mother Hen" to your children if you would let me. Little by little you released each finger that held on ever so tightly, learning to lean, learning to trust, knowing that I would not lie to you or fail you.

You went home with the picture, holding on to the promise I had given to you. I had even more to share with you from that picture. Early that morning before the funeral, you looked up and asked, "Father, somehow please let me know if my daddy is with you." Like years ago, before you called, I answered. In the middle of your question, I showed you the answer right before your eyes in that picture! You counted each chicken. There was one for every member of your household (family you had believed for in your heart). Not one was missing. Not even your daddy! There you were, like the little girl in the picture, giving them all to me.

One word from me was all you needed. You listened to My Voice. Another you would not follow. In a moment you knew beyond a shadow of a doubt that I was the keeper of all you had committed to Me years ago, the loved ones of your household, the ones whom you placed in the Ark, the safe Ark of the Covenant in your heart.

You knew I would express your love to your daddy. You would think I wish I had told Daddy "I love you" one more time. You wished you could have told him the words in your heart that were not so easily conveyed or expressed. You could have joy in your heart knowing that everything you ever wanted to express to your father, I would convey to him. I knew that was a deep desire of your heart and did I not tell you I give you the desires of the heart? I have shown him the natural love in your heart, but even more he has received by My Spirit the total fullness of My Covenant Love that is within you that knows no boundaries toward Heaven. My Covenant is the assurance that by faith, not one shall be missing.

The day of the funeral you did not see the casket or grave or the one whom you loved that was dead. You saw the picture on your wall: a picture of promise, a picture of truth. Your loved one was not in the grave, but alive walking and talking with me, fully understanding My Love and My Covenant because of My Precious Son's Blood.

All Your Children Shall Be Taught by Me

All your children shall be disciples [taught by the Lord] and [obedient to His will] and great shall be the peace and well-being of your children. Isaiah 54: 13

I am the Alpha and Omega, the beginning and the end. I am the Author and Finisher of your faith. I have said I am faithful to bring to pass my promises to you, "they are *yes* and *so be it*, because of My Dear Son, for My Name's sake." You can trust and rely on that. Look at Joseph. He said I had given him My Words, words I said I would be faithful to in his life. After I gave him My Words, he said, "because of faith, the Word of the Lord tried me. My feet were put in fetters because of God's words to me." The trial of Joseph's faith is more precious than gold. He was saying there was nothing he could do by himself. His feet were in stocks. My promises could happen only if I moved. He was faithful to believe I would bring it to pass in My way and in My time.

Believe Me when I say **all.** I say *all* your children will be taught by Me and their well-being and peace shall be not just okay or good, but great!

Paul had been tutored and taught by the best teachers and

was a very learned man. When he was on his way to Damascus I spoke and taught him. In one moment, My Word reorganized all his book learning of all those years. In Galatians I said, "It pleases me to reveal My Son to all your children; I will teach them. If they err, I will bring them back. I am their teacher!"

Your Children and Their Offspring Shall Eat at My Table Always

David said, Is there still anyone left of the house of Saul to whom I may show kindness and mercy for Jonathan's sake? 7) David said to him, Fear not, for I will surely show you kindness for Jonathan your father's sake and I will restore to you all the land of Saul, your father and grandfather and you shall eat at My table always. II Samuel 9: 1

How I desire for you to understand how My Covenant with you goes on and on, never ending. Let us talk about this situation with David and Jonathan. Years earlier David and Jonathan made covenant with one another. Their hearts were knitted together in My love. When Jonathan's life was over, the covenant lived on in David's heart. Years later David, his heart and mind on the covenant, asked the question, "Is there anyone left of the house of Saul to whom I may show kindness and mercy for Jonathan's sake? Where is he or she? I will go to them wherever they are in the earth."

Dear One, do you know that because of the covenant we have I continue to ask that same question concerning you and your household? After you are gone, I will go and do, for your sake and for Jesus' sake! What a better covenant we have now because of the Blood of My Dear Son. When I find your special one, I will surely show My kindness and mercy, just like I did when I found Jonathan's relative, Mephibosheth. I restored back to him the land which the enemy had stolen, the place I had in My mind and heart for him to possess. David brought Mephibosheth home to his house to live and told him he shall eat at his table always. Likewise, I will go and gather your children and your children's children and bring them to My house and feed them My Word as they sit at My table and eat. As David was faithful to Jonathan, how much more I, your Father God, Creator of Heaven, Earth and all mankind, will do all that I have sworn to you concerning My Covenant with you for Jesus' sake!

When It Pleases God

But when He, Who had chosen and set me apart [even] before I was born and had called me by His grace, saw fit and was pleased
16) to reveal His Son within Me I did not consult flesh and blood. Galatians 1:15, 16

Paul had sat at the feet of many learned teachers of the law of the old covenant. With his education he was doing what he thought was my bidding. Paul did not know I had chosen and set him apart even before he was born. In the fullness of time when it pleased Me by the Holy Spirit, I revealed My Son in him. He would never be the same after that day. He began that day to eat at my table, the steady, hearty menu of grace. It was not a menu of the law like he had been eating, but a table of grace and mercy. His appetite would grow bigger as the years would go by.

Likewise, Dear One, I will reveal My Covenant to you, and it will be birthed in the womb of your heart. As you sit at my table and eat My Words, that big round table keeps expanding with My love, mercy and grace.

There is an appointed time when it will please Me, to reveal My Son in your children. No flesh or blood could ever teach or reveal My Spirit to them. Your children are each unique and special to Me. I have a plan for all eternity for them. Trust Me that I will find each child on that road in life and I will be faithful to reveal My Son in them. A desire to know Me will be birthed in them and they too will say, "I have been delivered, I am being delivered and I shall be delivered even on that day."

I Am the Author and Source

They glorified God as the Author and Source of what had taken place in me. Galatians 1: 24

Only I can write the script in each of your lives to bring forth the good plans I have for you. I told you before the foundation of the world your name was written in the Book of Life and all the days of your life from birth to death are in there as well. I am truly, as My Word has spoken, your guide even until death.

When I reveal My Son by My Spirit in each of your children I will be glorified. In My perfect way and My perfect time I will be revealed as the Author and Source of what has taken place in them. Rest, rest in the love of My heart and the workings of My hands for each one. Trust Me, for My plans are well thought out!

I Will Pour Out My Spirit Upon Your Offspring

3) I will pour My spirit upon your offspring and My blessings upon your descendants.
4) They shall spring up among the grass like willows or poplars by the watercourses.
Isaiah 44:3,4

I did not say "sprinkle." Aren't you glad I will "pour" My Spirit and My blessings upon your offspring? This unique expression of My Love for each one will cause them to spring up by My Spirit. They will declare who they are in Me.

In sending My rain from heaven I will be like a gardener who knows when to water. I will pour just the right amount to cause each one to grow and flourish as they look to Me.

Do you remember how you and your neighbor Jayne delighted in this word concerning your children? Jayne had some beautiful willow trees planted by a running stream in her backyard. One year to her horror, she came home and her husband, Jerry, had pruned them severely down to the ground. She knew they could never possibly recover or come back. Jerry, who was a gardener assured her differently. She was heartsick.

You moved away. Seeing her again after several years you asked about the willow trees. It had not been too long until she looked out and there they were springing up in the grass, growing in the sun, being watered by the stream. They came back more beautiful than they had ever been.

Beloved, I am the great I Am. I Am here. I Am the great gardener of My Covenant. I care for and watch over My garden, your children, and the planting of the Lord. Even after I prune them they will come back and flourish, and be more beautiful than ever.

The Work of My Hands

Therefore, thus says the Lord, Who redeemed Abraham [out of Ur and idolatry] concerning the house of Jacob: Jacob shall not then be ashamed; not then shall his face become pale [with fear and disappointment because of his children's degeneracy.] 23) For when he sees his children [walking in the way of piety and virtue,] The Work of My Hands in his midst they will revere the Holy One of Jacob and reverently fear the God of Israel.
24) Those who err in Spirit will come to understanding and those who murmur [discontentedly] will accept instruction.
Isaiah 29 : 22

I have said over and over "There is none Righteous, no not one." This means you and your children. Because of this you can look at any of your children and at times be ashamed with fear and disappointment because of the sin in their life. You are disappointed in their actions, but even more you are disappointed in yourself. Somehow, the workings of your hands failed so the image of your mind is not present in your offspring. I spoke this word to the house of Jacob; I am also speaking loud and clear to you—the house of Linda. I established that I am the One who has the power and ability to redeem you and your children in the first place. Redemption is not meant to be your place, a mother's place. That is my part. At one time I had to redeem Abraham out of unrighteousness, the one with whom I would later covenant with and make the Father of many nations. With the Blood of My Dear Son, I have the power and ability to redeem the situation with your child. When you see the working of my hands, you will know it is the Lord your God who is working in the midst of your child's life. You will see or hear him honor and acknowledge Me. The prodigal Son's father had plenty to be fearful and ashamed about for a season, but he knew this promise. He knew the covenant I had with him concerning his house and his Son. I brought the son home after I had done a work in his heart because I knew his father had the son's robe and ring (My Covenant) waiting for him. The father and the son both honored Me for the working of my hands.

I Will Deliver — You Intercede

He will even deliver the one [for whom you intercede] who is not innocent; yes he will be delivered through the cleanliness of you hands. Job 22 : 30

    Have I told you that the blood of My Dear Son Jesus Christ not only saves and heals, but also delivers? Right now He is seated in Heaven at My right hand. My Word states his only job is to make intercession for you. I want you to see your self interceding on behalf of your children and your children's children. I have said, "Yes, I will deliver the one for whom you are praying, the one who is not innocent." Years ago I spoke to you about how to have clean hands. I said, "Linda wash your hands of this matter, let me do it with My hands." Immediately you saw that in order to wash your hands you had to put down anything you were holding. You must lay down your own plans, desires and thoughts for that child. After you wash your hands of your own workings and plans, your uplifted clean hands praised Me for the deliverance with full trust. Yes, I will deliver the one who is not clean, nor innocent, because of your intercession. You are standing in the gap. Oh, that I would find mothers standing in the gap for their children, releasing My hands to deliver them because of the promises of My Covenant.

I Give Light to You and Your Descendants

But the Lord would not destroy the house of David because He had made a covenant with David and promised to give a light to him and to his sons forever. II Chronicles 21: 7

You remember how darkness covered Egypt so completely that they could not see a thing right in front of their faces. During this time my people, the Israelites had light in their homes. You will have even more light in the spiritual realm because of My Covenant with David. My promise to him was not only to give a light to him, but to his sons forever. Even after David's body was laid in the ground My Promise continues.

My Dear One, Jesus My Son is the light of your heart. He lights up My Covenant of your heart to bring Me and My truth to you and to your offspring forever. As the darkness of satan grows darker and covers the earth, the god of this world seeks to steal, kill and destroy seeking whom he may devour. The world will not be able to see My light, even if I stand in front of their faces, because of the darkness in their hearts.

I will continue to bring the Light of My Salvation, Jesus, to you and to your household forever. I have promised. You have My Covenant!

I Will Bring Your Sons and Daughters from Afar

1) Fear not, for I have redeemed you ransomed you by paying a price instead of leaving you captives; I have called you by your name, you are mine.
5) Fear not, for I am with you, I will bring your offspring from the east where they are dispersed and gather you from the west.
6) I will say to the North–Give up and to the South, keep not back, bring My sons from afar and My daughters from the ends of the earth. Isaiah 43 : 1, 5, 6

I have not given you a spirit of fear, but a spirit of power, love, and a sound mind. Fear brings many raging voices which bring confusion and torment. I have said, "My people listen to Me, the Good Shepherd, the Bishop of their souls. My people do not follow another. They know My voice."

So fear not; before you were born I saw you. I looked at you your whole life and I saw the good and the bad. I called you by name. I saw you as a Pearl of Great Price. You are worth a great price because My Son in the fullness of time shed His blood for you. You are mine. By the power of My Spirit, I gently brought forth the Pearl within you, your Lord Jesus Christ who resides within you.

I told you to fear not over and over again when I said I will bring you to me in all power and authority because of faith in My Covenant with you. I will. I will also bring your offspring to me. From the ends of the earth, I will bring all My sons and daughters back to me.

My Son and I looked you over and counted the cost and declared you were worth it. So the high price for your total redemption was paid. Receive My Covenant for yourself and your children.

Your Sons and Daughters Shall Prophesy

And it shall come to pass in the last days, God declares, that I will pour out My spirit upon all mankind and your sons and your daughters shall prophesy. Acts 2:17

    I declare unto you, I will pour, not sprinkle, but pour out My Spirit in the last days and your sons and daughters shall prophesy! Out of their mouths they shall speak My Words. They will marvel, as well as those around them who hear. It may be a word or two, but one word anointed by My Spirit is powerful. I will send a word to a receptive heart to set the captives free, to bring salvation to a lost soul. I will send healing to their bodies or speak My plans and purposes to them. I will touch a wayward soul who has lost his way. In a moment your sons and daughters shall speak. Their words will go forth and accomplish My will and plans in the earth.

    Believe this Dear One, for your sons and daughters. Believe what I say I will do. It is My Covenant!

Have Confidence in Me Concerning Your Children

3) Yet the Lord is faithful and He will strengthen you and set you on a firm foundation and guard you from the evil One.
4) And we have confidence in the Lord concerning you . . .
II Thessalonians 3:3,4

    In Revelation as I ride forth, I am called Faithful and True! In whatever situation or circumstance you may find yourself, you can know that I will be faithful to you. I cannot deny who I am or be anything but true to you.

    Abraham knew I would be faithful to him and would bring to pass what I said I would do. Can you believe me for the same? As you wait on the fulfillment of My promises in My Word, I will strengthen you. Faith is not of yourself, but of Me. Just ask for it. Just receive it. It is yours. There is a firm foundation that is built on the death and resurrection of My Son Jesus Christ. I will set you on that firm foundation that everything else is built upon. It will not crack, leak or crumble. Yes, Jesus is the chief cornerstone of My House. My house is a sure house. Know that as I build this house I will guard it and you from the evil One. That is why I declare to you over and over not to fear.

You have been interceding for your children. Receive My Words of promise over them. Always remember Beloved, do not ever put your confidence in them or in their flesh, be it good or bad. Let your confidence always be in Me concerning them. Yet, remember while they may be unfaithful, I will remain faithful. I cannot let you down. I am the Faithful One!

I Will Make for You a House

11)... The Lord declares to you that He will make for you a house:
12) And when your days are fulfilled and you sleep with your fathers, I will set up after you your offspring who shall be born to you, and I will establish his kingdom.
16) Your house and your kingdom shall be made sure forever before you; Your throne shall be established forever.
28) Now, O Lord God, You are God and Your words are truth, and you have promised this good thing to your servant.
29) therefore now let it please you to bless the house of your servant that it may continue forever before you; For you, O Lord God, have spoken it, and with Your blessing let his house be blessed forever.   II Samuel 7 : 11-29

Oh Dear Precious One, look at what I declare to you, I will make for you a house. I alone am the builder of your house, a sure house that will not crumble or fall.

I will find and establish the house of your offspring after you, because of the promise I have declared to you. Remember I am the Creator and Builder of the whole universe. Can I create and build your house? I have said in My Word that the Holy Spirit and I desire a resting place, a place where we can reside and establish our Kingdom within you. When asked of Jesus by the disciples

"Where is the Kingdom of Heaven?" did I not respond, the Kingdom of Heaven is within you? It is written that the Kingdom of Heaven is righteousness, joy, peace and fellowship in the Holy Spirit. That is the sure house that I desire to build for you. My Son's blood allows you to stand rightly before Me. It is His righteousness in you that makes you clean before Me. When I build My righteousness within you, it brings joy and peace and immediate fellowship with Me that calms all your anxieties and fears. I begin in your heart as your King. Little by little, I become the Head of the home within you. More and more you will know, understand and behold I am God and My Words are true. I have promised this to you.

It pleases Me to bless your house that it may continue forever. I have spoken it. This is My Covenant with you!

I Am the Builder and Furnisher

Every house is built and furnished by someone, but the Builder of all things and the Furnisher of the entire equipment of all things is God. Hebrews 3 : 4

I want to lay the Cornerstone, My Son Jesus, to be the solid foundation of your house to hold everything together. I want to gently build line upon line, precept upon precept, here a little, there a little. I desire to build your house and furnish it. Yes, furnish and fill it up so that you and I might rest in it.

You see, this house is being built in your heart. I will furnish it with My love, joy and peace if you will let me. Until now you have not asked anything in My name. Ask that your joy may be full. I have come that you may be saved and have eternal life, but also have life more abundant. I want to build and fill up your house to overflowing, a sure house with all the fullness of My love, My joy and My peace. I want to fill you with Me, forever. This is My Covenant with you!

Except I Build the House

Except the Lord build the house they labor in vain that build it.
Psalm 127 : 1

Here I am building your house again. You have realized by now the working of your own hands has been to no avail. I have said in My Word a wise woman builds her house with a heart of faith and trusts Me to be the Builder and Furnisher of her house. A foolish woman tears it down with the working of her own hands. Have I not said I want to dress you in white fine linen which causes no sweat? Resting in me. Oh, Dear One, why do you want to keep putting on wool clothing that causes sweat and anxiety by your own thoughts and workings? Well, every mother and grandmother has to fight the good fight of faith in this area over her household by allowing me to build her house. Let the workings of your hands be burned up. There have to be ashes before I can give My everlasting beauty; mourning before I can give My eternal joy. Because of My love for you, Beloved, I will come in and tear down all that you try to build out of the wisdom of your own mind. I will rebuild My eternal home in your heart. My Son is now preparing and building that house for you, His Bride, that is full and furnished with peace, love, joy and happiness forever. I am building even now a measure of that same house within you.

I must build the house. Cease from your own labors and let Me be the Builder. This is My Covenant with you!

The Child Shall Be a Nazarite

... the child shall be a Nazarite to God from birth to the day of His death! Judges 13 : 7

The story and life of Samson have brought living truths of My Covenant over your children to you! Before Samson was born I sent My Word through an Angel to tell Samson's mother that this child shall be a Nazarite, a child of covenant from birth to the day of his death! I made a promise to his mother that no matter what would transpire in this precious one's life, He was marked with My Covenant. I called him by name. He is mine. He is a covenant child! That is right. When I saw him rolling in his natal blood and his mother's umbilical cord had yet to be cut, I beheld him and looked and said, "Live Samson—Live. You shall not die but live and declare the illustrious acts of Me." Before Samson was born, his father asked the angel two questions as he prayed. "Oh Lord, teach us what we shall do with the child that shall be born." He prayed and asked also, "Lord, show us how we shall manage this child." Both times I gave to the mother the answer. My answer was to keep your heart pure and full of faith in My Covenant with you concerning this child. What I have spoken about him is true. I will be faithful to you concerning Samson. I will be Mother Hen over him. The storms may rage but My Word over your child has made a sure house in you. In the end it will still be standing when all other pillars fall.

After Samson was born, he grew and I blessed him and My Spirit moved him. You know the story of how Samson went out of the camp down to the good looking Philistine women who were young girls not of the covenant. Samson said, "They all look all right in my eyes." Samson's mother and father tried to talk him out of marrying one of these girls as they knew she was not of My Covenant. Could not he marry a girl of the covenant? They tried to tell him he was unequally yoked to a wrong girl.

Your eyes were opened in the next scripture where I wrote, "His father and mother did not know it was of the Lord." Looking at Samson's life and his flesh after this point looks disastrous. It was disastrous, but I had given a promise. I had sworn to his mother and father My Covenant over this child.

They could wholly give this child to Me forever. I am faithful and true. All I had asked of the mother from the beginning was to keep her heart pure no matter what she may see, hear or experience in this child's life. Do not let your heart or emotions be contaminated with the enemy's lies or with the many voices in the world. Keep your heart pure with My Word of Truth to you. I have spoken it. Shall I not also do it?

Samson, bowed and humbled himself mightily in the end of his life. He called to Me and said, "Oh Lord God, remember me I pray to you, and strengthen me."

I heard his cry and I allowed more of his enemies to be slain at his death than in his life. To many people Samson's life is thought of only as a disaster, but if you read in My book of Hebrews, My heroes of faith, Samson is there. Many mothers would love to see their son's name written in stone for all eternity as a Hero of Faith.

Oh, keep your heart pure, full of trust, Beloved, believing Me. That is how to teach and manage your child, from birth until death. This child shall be a Nazarite to Me. A child of a covenant promise!

Your Children Around Your Table

3)... Your children shall be like olive plants around about your table.
6) Yes, May you see your children's children...Psalm 128: 3, 6

I am the Lord your God who chose you, loved you, and sought after you. You Dear One, the one whom I chose and brought out of a place where you did not know Me. You did not know My love or My faithfulness for you. I have brought you out of the house inside you where I was not a guest. I never wanted to be an unseen guest. I want to be One who is seen, heard and listened to; One who can guide and speak to your life. I want to be as close and near as anyone in the family. I am all wise and care for you and your household.

Early one morning you were preparing dinner and setting the big round oak table with your fine linen and china. As you set the table you decided not only to put places for the four of you, but you set a place for Me. There were five places. You thought when the family all came in they would want to know who the guest would be for dinner. Late that afternoon everything was set. You thought the only thing missing was a fresh beautiful bouquet of flowers for the table. The phone rang and your neighbor Mary said, "Linda come over, I want to give you something." When you walked in her home you saw a beautiful arranged bouquet of flowers she had just received for her birthday. They were going out of town and she wanted to give them to you. You wept because you knew those gorgeous flowers were from Me. I had sent them to you, my Beloved. As your family came in they each asked, "Hey who is coming to dinner and where did those flowers come from?" What great delight you had in telling them!

In My Word I have asked, where can I find a heart that is faithful in the earth? Where is a heart that I can sit with around the table and make covenant, as I speak the Word of My Covenant. As we sit and sup together, as we share My Word, the very flowers will appear. You know I do all things well and fulfill My Word to you. The table has been set. The meal complete. The flowers are in place. Partake of all of Me; taste and see that My Covenant is good. I will hiss for your children and call to them. One by one I will cause them to come and sit at My table. They will ask "Who is here for dinner and where did the flowers come from?" They will come into My fullness.

I will fulfill My promise for I am just and righteous. This is My Covenant!

Your Children Shall Be Established Before Me

The children of your servants shall dwell safely and continue, and their descendants shall be established before you.
Psalm 102 : 28

What a joy flooded your heart the day you saw what I had done in the life of Job. In the beginning of Job it is written that he had a designated number of animals. Each kind of animal and the exact number of each is listed. At the end I gave the number of children, the exact number of sons and daughters.

You read how his sons and daughters and animals were killed through a disaster. Many do not read the end of the story. In the end I doubled the numbers of each animal he had in the beginning, but gave not a double number, but a single number of sons and daughters. What joy you experienced when you realized there was no mistake in the numbers. You realized that day, they *had* been doubled, only the first seven children were with Me! I had been faithful to Job and My Covenant over Job's household. His children would continue and are established, set even this day for all eternity in My Covenant!

The blood of My Dear Son, Jesus has set forth My Covenant

over you and your household. For all eternity your sons and daughters shall continue and be established before Me.

This is My Covenant! I was faithful to Job under the old covenant. How much more I will be faithful to you, Dear One, under My New Covenant.

My Righteousness to Your Children's Children

The mercy and loving kindness of the Lord are from everlasting to everlasting upon those who reverently and worshipfully fear Him, and His righteousness is to children's children.
Psalm 103:17

    My mercy and loving kindness endures forever. They will endure through every situation. In the book of Psalms, David wrote frequently about this statement. He needed My mercy and loving kindness for his life. When My children, the Israelites had sinned, I was about to judge them harshly. Moses, with all boldness, reminded Me of My mercy and loving kindness toward My children. I relented and acknowledged My great mercy and loving kindness in that situation. In My Word I have said, "Mercy triumphs over Judgment." When sin is recognized and confessed at the Judgment Seat of Christ, My Dear Son, His blood cleanses and washes as white as snow every spot and stain. My Son's blood was not and never will be in vain in your life. It shall endure forever. Because of My Covenant of Righteousness, which represents right standing with Me, it is promised to your children's children. I have said, I will teach them. They will know My Righteousness. They will understand all about coming and standing before Me. I will never shut the door in their faces or turn away. I will listen to them and I will talk with them. If I chastise them on occasion it is because I have told them they are mine. As a loving Father, I care about them and desire the best. I want to keep them from evil and from going down the wrong paths. My chastisement will always be covered with My mercy and loving kindness. My chastisement is never a beating but a training. I train those I love. You and your children will reign with Me, in mercy, loving kindness and righteousness.

This is My Covenant!

You and Your Children' Children Shall Dwell in the Land

They shall dwell in the Land in which your fathers dwelt, that I gave to My servant Jacob and they shall dwell there, they and their children's children, forever; and My servant David shall be their Prince forever. Ezekiel 37 : 25

As you know, the land in the Old Testament was a physical natural land. The land I bring you, your children, and your children's children into is a spiritual place, a land to occupy in the heart. As the day approaches, My Beloved, that you have longed for and looked to, My appearing nears. I have said, "Occupy until I come." Some see that as business as usual in the physical, natural sense. Some will be too busy occupying, running here and there, buying, selling and building. Yes, even their ministry will occupy them. Beloved, let my desire be your desire. Occupy all the land I have promised you. Let Me be who I am in you and you be who you are in Me. Let Me, My Son and My Holy Spirit come in and occupy our whole house within your heart. I want you to dwell in a house that hands did not build. I want you to have a land like Abraham said he was looking for, a land and city whose builder and maker is Me. Let Me build a land in your heart that is occupied with My love, My joy and My peace. This is My promise to you, your children and your children's children forever!

David in the Old Testament was a type of My Son Jesus, the

Prince of Peace, who was to come and has come. Jesus being the Root of David, sprang forth in the fullness of time to bring My New Covenant with all its better promises in the land. My servant David shall be your prince forever, through Jesus Christ, who is head of your house and land forever.

This is My Covenant!

Guard and Keep these Truths

Guard and keep with the greatest care the precious and excellent Truth which has been entrusted to you by the Holy Spirit Who makes His home in us. II Timothy 1 : 14

    This was My Word to My son Timothy through Paul. This is My word to you, Beloved. I want you to guard your heart with the greatest care. The truth of My Covenant is being written to you in this book. I have come to you by the power of My Holy Spirit who makes His home in you. I want you to keep the doors and even the little windows of your heart shut to any words that might oppose My Truth that has been entrusted to you. I want you to know the Precious seed of My Word has been sown in good soil in your heart by My Holy Spirit. Satan, your adversary, comes immediately to kill, steal and destroy what Precious truth I have planted within you. Stand firm, hold on, keep allowing Me to nurture that seed of My Word within you. Satan will come knocking at the door asking, "May I steal that word from you?" He wants you to look at your circumstances, trying to convince you My Word is not true in your case. Do not listen to him. Guard and keep it like your most precious possession. It will not disappoint you. As I have said even though My Word at the moment be like the smallest of seeds, the mustard seed, let me water and feed it. Do not let it go. I promise it will grow little by little into a mighty shade tree not only for you to find refuge, but for others to come find peace, rest and a place to lay their weary souls in one of my branches.

Be patient, My Dear One, it takes time for a tree to grow. As you guard My Truth and as you watch and wait, One day you will see, first a shoot, then a trunk, then a branch with beautiful green shade leaves. This will be a planting of Me that will be forever and ever.

This is My Covenant!

My Majesty to Your Children

Let your work, the signs of your power, be revealed to your servants, and your glorious majesty to our children.
Psalm 90 : 16

Let Me work with the workings of My hands in your life and in your children. I said in My Word, it is not by your might, nor by your power, but by My Spirit. You can remember when Trevor, your son, was in high school playing baseball and you watched as he stood on base and a fellow ran into him. He was rushed to a hospital in Atlanta where he had intricate surgery on a nerve in his elbow at two o'clock in the morning, so he would have use of his arm. The surgery went well, but he could not straighten out his arm. The doctors suggested that after much physical therapy he *might* have use of his arm again. Before his first visit to the therapist all of you went to a church meeting. Trevor went down for prayer for his arm. On the way home he looked at his Dad and said "Look, look at my arm!" He held it out perfectly straight. Before the prayer all he could do was hold it bent at the elbow. I had shown My Power, My Work and My Glorious Majesty to you and to your son that night. You glorified Me then and you are even now, by relating this all over again.

All Trevor has is a small faint scar under his elbow. What a wondrous sign of remembrance for him when things in his life get tough and it seems like his life is in a whirlwind. He, like

David, will know that "I remembered." So your child can remember I am with him, I am at work in his life, and I am the One who in the end does all things well. You and he have learned to trust Me.

This is My Covenant!

Your Children's Children

5) May the Lord bless you out of Zion [His sanctuary] and may you see the prosperity of the Lord all the days of your life.
6) Yes, may you see your children's children. Peace be upon you.
Psalm 128 : 5,6

    I have told you over and over, "I Am Love." Read the Love chapter in Corinthians that describes Me, out of Zion, My sanctuary, which is My heart of Love. My desire is to bless you and your children with prosperity. I am the One who thought this up. My desire from the beginning, the desire of the ages, is to prosper you in this way. Prosperity to the world is in money and power. Money cannot buy and power cannot obtain what is truly valuable. Money is cold and power is lonely. There is never a U-Haul behind a hearse and even powerful men are soon forgotten. Wood, hay and stubble will soon burn up. Only that which is of Me shall remain. Prosperity and blessing that are eternal have the weight of gold. You see, in this Word of mine, I ask you if I may bless you. May I open your heart and eyes to let you see my real true prosperity, not just for an hour or a day, but for all the days of your life. I want you to have a full prosperous life of knowing Me, a loving Father, who will never, never leave you or forsake you. I will not relax My hold on you even for a second. I love and care for you as the "Apple of My Eye." This is My heart's desire for you and your children. In this word you can see that the blessing you want more than anything the world has to offer would be to see your children and your children's children in My care. You see, I have said an emphatic "yes." May you see your children's children. I say to you "This is My desire. May I bless you with this?" Peace be upon you in knowing you have this request.

This is My Covenant!

Your Children Will Not Beg for Bread

I have been young and now am old, yet I have not seen the righteous forsaken or their children begging bread.
Psalm 36 : 25

What a promise, what wonderful assurance to you! You can count on it. First of all, you know you are My Righteousness. You have been forgiven, cleansed and made righteous by My Son's blood. I have said I do not forsake My own. As you look back on different situations, maybe wondering where I was in the middle of them, *I was right there*. It is no light promise of mine when I have said in My word, "I will never, no never, forsake you or relax My hold on you." You are secure in Me. My Word concerning your children is here. They shall not beg for bread. I am the Bread of Life, the bread sent from Heaven that satisfies the soul and fulfills the hunger. Your children do not need to beg Me for what is rightfully theirs.

The Gentile mother came and asked me to minister deliverance to her daughter. I replied that I had come only to those of the Covenant. At that point I said it is not fair to give Bread (the promise of My Covenant) to others because it belongs to My children. As faith rose up in her she asked for the crumbs from the bread that had fallen from the table. I could not deny her faith. I responded, "O woman, great is your faith! Be it done for you as you wish." Her daughter was cured from that moment. I could not forsake or deny her because of her faith. According to your faith, so shall it be!

How you rejoiced when you saw in My Word where a person who needed ministry went to a friend during the midnight hour of his life. When he got there, he was told, "I of myself have nothing to give, but I know someone who is able to meet your need." He brought his friend to My house and knocked on My door. I told him from inside My door that I was resting and My Bread was only for My children. I had a responsibility to meet the needs of the children of the covenant. Just because he was a friend did not mean he should receive anything. Because of his persistence in knocking to receive the Bread of My Covenant, I could not resist his faith. I opened My door to him, and I will open it for you, Dear One. As I opened it he asked Me for three loaves of bread to minister to his body, soul and spirit. The three loaves of bread also represent Us, who created the Universe, Father God, Son Jesus, and the Holy Spirit. We were the three loaves of bread he was asking for. I could not resist his faith in pursuing the promises of My Covenant. I said, "Because of this great faith, so be it!" Beloved, so be it to you. Your children shall not be out begging for bread. The three loaves of bread are prepared for them, whether their needs are body, soul, or spirit. I am the Bread of life that was broken for them. Do not be denied. Knock on My door. It may be the midnight hour, but I will answer. I will be there to serve with My three loaves of bread on my silver platter of redemption. I came into the world not to be served but to serve. I love you. I love your children. I love your children's children.

This is My Covenant!

I Will Give Increase to You and Your Children

May the Lord give you increase more and more, you and your children. Psalm 115 : 14

My Beloved, My child, John the Baptist, said the words, "I must decrease that He (Jesus) might increase." Oh, how you have learned little by little that as your thoughts, your own plans, your own ways, decrease, My thoughts, My plans increase in your mind and life. I desire for you to renew your mind by laying down all your wrong thoughts and filling it with what I say to you. You must decrease so I can increase. My ways, My thoughts, are not your thoughts. My ways are higher. To come up higher in your thinking is to deny your own thoughts and sit with me in heavenly places. Then you can look down at a situation and see what I am doing from My perspective. Oh, that you would come higher more and more. That is what I desired for My children from the very beginning. I wanted Adam and Eve to continue being keepers in the beautiful garden I had given them, so we could walk and talk in the cool of that garden. I wanted them to have a full forever-increasing peaceful life in the home I had prepared for them. Satan, the evil one, caused them to question My intent, My care, My love in their minds. The Father of lies (for there is no truth in him) lied and deceived them when he said they would increase in knowledge if they would only listen to his words and obey them. As you know, Adam and Eve chose to be increased that day, while they ate of the tree of knowledge of Good and Evil. It was fulfilling and tasty for the moment, but robbed, stole and deceived them for the rest of their lives and many generations after them.

My son Jesus has come and paid the price for the restoration of all things in your life and your children. That is good news to you, Dear One. I never meant for you to desire an increase in worldly things and pleasures of life. This must decrease. I want you to increase in knowing Me, having fellowship with Me. Increase by being filled with My spirit, so you can know my purpose and plan for your life. This is My Covenant, that you, your children and your children's children would increase more and more in My Covenant.

Promise of The Holy Spirit to You and Your Children

For the promise of the Holy Spirit is to and for you and your children and to and for all that are far away . . . Acts 2 : 39

In the beginning of creation I said, "Let us make man in our image". The "us" is the three: Father, Son and Holy Spirit. We have been from the beginning. I sent My Son, Jesus, to die that you might live forever and have all things restored back to you that satan had stolen. My Son, Jesus Christ, is seated at my right hand and his only job at this moment is to forever intercede on your behalf and to prepare a place for you. All that you ask of Me according to My Word, it is granted in His Name. I will give you those desires of your heart for all eternity.

In Acts I told those who were mine to go and wait until they receive power from My Holy Spirit. He would be the one who would be their teacher. He would be their Comforter. He would draw them to Me. He would convict them of their sin that they might live peaceful whole lives. Even Mary, the Mother of My Son, needed to be with the ones who waited to receive the power of the Holy Spirit to indwell her being. Even though Mary had conceived My Son by the Holy Spirit, even though I had breathed on her later in her life, it wasn't until the Holy Spirit was sent that she received the empowering of the Third Person of Heaven.

My Beloved, through My Word, this promise that was given to Mary and the disciples back then is still for you today. If Jesus, My Son, depended on the power of the Holy Spirit, how much more My children from His seed need it. Ask for it! Know it is now that you receive Him. Expect Him to empower you. He will hear from Me and speak to your heart what I tell him through Jesus, your Savior, your Advocate, your Intercessor, your High Priest.

The wonderful promise is that it is not only to you Dear One, but it is to your children, even those who might be far away from Me in their hearts. My powerful Holy Spirit has defeated the unholy spirit. The power that defeated satan and raised Christ from the dead dwells in you. You have power in you to defeat the obstacles in life and the enemies to your soul! Believe me to send that same power to seek out, find and bring back your children and empower their lives.

This is My Covenant.

I Will Save You and Your Offspring

Fear not, and be not dismayed, for behold, I will save you from afar, and your offspring from the land of their exile, and Jacob will return and be quiet and at ease and none will be afraid.
Jeremiah 46 : 27

Oh Precious One, over and over I tell mine not to fear or be dismayed when troubling certain situations or circumstances seem to invade their lives. I have not given you a Spirit of fear but of power, love and a sound mind. When you leave your fear behind and return to me in your heart and mind, quietness and confidence shall be your strength. I will, as a good shepherd, lead you by still waters and quiet resting places. In me there is rest.

You remember the story well when My servant Elijah was fearful and running for his life and hiding in a cave. I came to him not in a loud thunderous way, but in a quiet still voice. I asked, "What are you doing running scared like this?" He was in a far country, running physically and in his emotions and mind. But, oh what My still small voice can do to bring a heart back home again from a far country. I have promised you and your offspring. I will do it. Out of the abundance of the heart the mouth speaks. Over and over, My great exceeding Precious promises I speak to you out of the abundance of My Heart with My Mouth. Know that when you return to listen to My Words you can be quiet, be at ease, and not be afraid. This is My Covenant!

Come Have Breakfast

Jesus said to them "Come have breakfast." John 21: 12

Three powerful words I am speaking here! Over twenty years ago you heard these three words and saw My Son, Jesus, in a new and living way. Your Dear friend, Dolly, and you were at a meeting hearing a man speak about Jesus and Peter on the seashore. Peter knew Jesus was coming to see him. After Peter had failed and was crushed that he had denied Jesus, he wept over it. Jesus had told him earlier he was going to experience a failure in his life, but Jesus would be praying that He would not lose faith through this failure, this set back in life. Jesus prayed he would know that He could trust that I am still in control. I still love him and nothing can separate Me from him.

My Son, Jesus, told Peter that after he would fail and deny him that he would also strengthen the brethren from this situation. By the suffering he would experience, he would know of My forgiveness, mercy and everlasting love that no failure could ever destroy. Peter learned that while his flesh was weak in trying to walk after me, I would work in his life. He received power by My Spirit at Pentecost.

You and Dolly sat there hearing my words of encouragement

for your own lives from Peter's experience. All of a sudden you heard these three words "COME EAT BREAKFAST." The words of the speaker were like shouted from Heaven in your heart. All of a sudden, you knew Me and My Son in a way you had never known us before. Peter had already heard I wanted to see him. Yes, Peter had failed me, but My love was going after him. He had lied and denied me that night. My Son suffered and bled his Precious cleansing blood, and died and was resurrected from the grave of death. You saw me on the seashore calling to Peter. He was whom My Son had died for, and for all of those after him who would fail me. I will be there to strengthen them and tell them not to lose faith in Me. They must go from that experience and strengthen others in life who would also fail and be sorrowful. You saw My Son cooking fish on the coals of fire for Peter and the disciples. You thought how can Jesus, Son of God, Savior of the World, be cooking? Doesn't He know there are lost souls needing to be saved, sick and dying people that need to be delivered and healed? But Jesus is cooking. He only has a few days on this earth before He goes to His Father. He is cooking fish. Then he calls to Peter by name, (you see he hasn't forgotten His Chosen One, the Apple of His Eye) "Peter Come Eat Breakfast." He was saying to Peter you stood by these coals of fire once before and here they are again. That was at a midnight hour in your life when all seemed lost. Weeping was for the night, but Joy comes in the morning. "Peter, the Sun is coming up. I am here. It is the beginning of a new day for you! Come Eat Breakfast." They were told to break the fast. Come and dine with me. If you notice at the breakfast table. I didn't even bring up Peter's failure. I knew his heart. I wanted him to go forth and feed My lambs and strengthen them in My Love and My Forgiveness.

A seed of My Word was planted in your heart that night! All you wanted to talk to your friend Dolly about were those three words, "Come Eat Breakfast." I would continue to water these words and they would grow in a wonderful way. Years later you saw the big picture of "The Lord's Supper" your mother and brother put on the wall of your childhood home. All your life you had seen the table, the loaves of bread, the goblets of wine. To your amazement there on that table were plates of fish. What tears of joy! You saw those fish that would say days later, it is morning time, a new day of beginnings, forget those things which are behind. You saw the fish. How could you have missed it. They had been on the table all these years. Now you began to see them. You saw My only Son, the "Apple of Mine Eye" was laying down His life before His disciples breaking the bread (His Body) and drinking of the wine out of the cup (His Blood). On the table were those "apples" representing to you the "Apple of Mine Eye," the joy of you to our Hearts. You saw the little plates of fish where we say to you Dear One, "Come Eat Breakfast!" I reveal this to your heart, and to the hearts of your children and your children's children. This table is what my redemption for you and your household is all about.

Set this table for your family. Show them my love and forgiveness in a new and living way. All I asked Peter to do was "feed My lambs." I want you to feed your family my words of forgetting those things which are behind and partaking of the life ahead in Me. A new morning, a new Breakfast! Come and eat. This is My Covenant!

Your Sons and Daughters Shall be Recovered

3) David and his men came to the town, and behold, it was burned, and their wives and sons and daughters were taken captive.
6) David was greatly distressed for the men spoke of stoning him because the souls of them all were bitterly grieved, each man for his sons and daughters. But David encouraged and strengthened himself in the Lord his God.
8) And David inquired of the Lord, saying, shall I pursue this troop? Shall I overtake them? The Lord answered him, Pursue! For you shall surely overtake them and without fail recover all.
18) David recovered all that the Amalekites had taken and rescued his two wives.
19) Nothing was missing, small or great, sons or daughters spoil of anything that had been taken; David recovered all!
I Samuel 30:3,6,8,18,19.

David, a man after My own heart, had many trials and tribulations. In this world you shall have trials and tribulations. You are mine. I have told you to be of good cheer, because whatever trial of your faith has distressed you, I have already overcome. I already know the outcome and My blessing will come. I promise this to you.

In order for to walk this out in your own life, you must see the steps David took. First you may look in your household to see where satan, the adversary, has sought to rob physically or spiritually One or all in your household, those you are holding in faith. Do not allow this heart-wrenching situation to cause you distress. Learn from David. Move on to My provision for you. Encourage and strengthen yourself in Me, the Lord your God. Go back to this covenant. Eat My Covenant and My Promises over and over. Get strength from My Word. I am My Word.

The next step is to inquire of Me about the person, or the situation to know how to pray and intercede for your family that has been captured. I will show you how you can pray for their return. I say to you "pursue" in your prayers. My Son will make intercession for you and will take your words and desires and bring them boldly to Me. Because of His Blood, I can say to you, you will recover all. None shall be missing on that day!

This is My Covenant!

Your Descendants Will Be Delivered

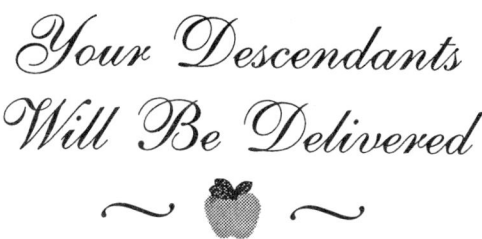

Assuredly, the evil man will not go unpunished. But the descendants of the righteous will be delivered. Proverbs 11:21

Beloved, My Word declares you can have assurance in what I say. I am the Deliverer, the One who delivered Israel and the One who delivers you. I say to you that your descendants will be delivered. I deliver and take out a stony, cold heart and put in My warm heart of love and care.

The whole world lies under the power of the evil one. There are many in the world who continue to listen to his words and his thoughts. They continue to do his deeds. They will not go unpunished because they have never listened to Me. They missed My Words of redemption to their souls through the price and punishment put on My Son, Jesus Christ.

Did I not say that your punishment for your sin, no matter how horrible, was laid upon Him who knew no sin that you could become My righteousness? That is what makes you righteous, Beloved. I declare that your descendants will be delivered!

This is My Covenant!

Your Children Are My Heritage and My Reward

Behold children are a heritage of the Lord and the fruit of the womb is His reward. Psalm 127 : 3

I want you to look at this word in awe. This is important. Oh, this is so important. Do you realize that your children are my inheritance? Did I not say I knew them, called them by name, had plans for their lives, since before the foundation of the earth? They were a seed in My heart that I allowed to be planted in you to bring forth My joy and My delight. We have shared together the awesomeness of birth. You, like Hannah, gave them to Me, trusting Me with their very lives for all eternity. I let you know I would watch over, water, and care for My seed. My inheritance and My heritage are in that Precious child. It is no light matter that I sent My only son to bleed and die on your child's behalf.

All the fruit of the Spirit, the love, joy, peace, longsuffering and patience, are developed and brought forth in the heart of your child. This is of Me, it is My reward. I desire many sons and daughters who are just like Me, created in My image and My likeness. I am the Potter at the wheel bringing forth those vessels of honor. Because of My Covenant, those children are My fruit, My heritage, My workmanship. I want you to see them as My vessels of honor even though right now you see their feet of clay. See them in My spirit and not in the flesh.

I will be faithful in what I say to you. As a branch that abides in the vine, they shall bear much fruit. They will be presented to Me blameless without spot or blemish by My Son, Jesus. The perfect Lamb of Mine laid down His life that they might live forever. They are mine! They are My heritage and My reward.

This is My Covenant!

Your Offspring Shall Endure Forever

28) My mercy and loving kindness will I keep for him forevermore, and My Covenant shall stand fast and be faithful with him.
29) His offspring also will I make to endure forever, and his throne as the days of heaven.
30) If his children forsake My law and walk not in My ordinances.
31) If they break or profane My statues and keep not My commandments.
32) Then will I punish their transgression with the rod of chastisement and their iniquity with stripes.
33) Nevertheless, My loving kindness will I not break off from him, nor allow My faithfulness to fail [to lie to him.]
34) My covenant I will not break nor alter the thing that is gone out of My lips.
35) Once for all I have sworn by My holiness, which cannot be violated; I will not lie to David.
36) His offspring shall endure forever, and his throne shall continue as the sun before Me.
37) It shall be established forever as the moon, the faithful witness in the heavens.
Selah [pause and calmly think on that]! Psalm 89 : 28

My mercy and loving kindness endure forever. Because of the blood of My Son in bringing My New Covenant, My mercy triumphs over judgement. My covenant over your children was My idea. It was not and never has been your idea. I have sworn to you by My holiness, that My Covenant cannot be annulled or violated. I did not lie to David and I will not lie to you. Your children might forsake My way for them or might not keep My Commandment. As a loving Father and as a Good Shepherd who cares for His own, I will lovingly and gently rebuke and chastise them for My sake, their sake, and your sake.

I have told you if I do not do that, they are like thrown away orphans about whom no one cares. Your children are not of the sort. They are covenant children. They are marked. They shall be prophets and priests unto Me forever. This is established in Heaven and the Earth. I will mold and make them. I will work to form and do in your children for My good pleasure. My desire is to do them good in the end, to make them into strong overcomers in Me. The battle is mine and the victory is Mine. As they slowly and gently die to self through the experiences of life, they will also say, "I have heard with the hearing of My ears, but now I know face to face."

Beloved, look up every morning and behold the beautiful sun or in the evening the shining of the moon. Look up, do not look around. Everyday this is the promise of My faithfulness and My Covenant to you. It never fails. Even the days when there are overcast or cloudy skies to conceal the sun, it is there. I promise you, it is there.

This is My Covenant! Clouds within your life may have concealed My Covenant from your eyes, but it is forever shining in you heart and mine. Sit and think about this!

Companionship and Participation

God is Faithful (reliable, trustworthy, and therefore, ever true to His promise, and He can be depended on); by Him you were called into companionship and participation with His Son, Jesus Christ our Lord! I Corinthians 1 : 9

I am the Faithful One, faithful to you Beloved. You were called before the foundation of the world to be My companion for life. I want us to walk together and talk together daily. We will have relationship. Relationship that comes from spending time together, from Me talking and you listening, you talking and Me listening. I desire My heartbeat would be your heartbeat; My thoughts would be your thoughts, My words would be your words.

My Son, Jesus Christ, your Lord has this relationship with Me. He clearly said, "I only do what I see My Father doing and I only speak what I hear My Father speaking." As Father and Son, we participated together in the earth bringing forth many brethren for Him, and many sons and daughters for Me. Oh, what a family I have because of His obedient participation. Even though a Son, a perfect Son from the very beginning, He learned obedience form the things which He suffered in the earth. He knew out of that suffering would be a training to reign forever. It would be worth it all. The joy that was set before Him, after the suffering, would be forever.

Come away My Beloved from the cares of the day and sit and let us have sweet fellowship and companionship. We can really get to know one another by spending time together. In doing this, the intercession of My Son, Jesus, becomes your intercession; therefore whatever you bind on earth shall be bound in heaven, whatever you loose on earth shall be loosed in heaven. My thoughts shall become your thoughts; My ways your ways. We are one and shall become one forever.

You are listening to Me and speaking and bringing forth My Covenant to hearts on the earth. My desire has become your desire. You are participating with My Dear Son, Jesus Christ, your Brother and Lord. Ultimately, you are participating with your God, the I AM who made you My idea. My very self is in you, My Seed!

This is My Covenant!

My Children Living in the Truth

I have no greater joy than this, to hear that My Children are living their lives in the Truth. III John 1:4

Oh, how I love the praises of My children. I love to hear their prayers. I love to see them study and receive My Word. I rejoice when they share with others what they have received. I rejoice when the gifts of My Spirit are operating in their lives. This all brings Me great joy. I have no greater joy than to hear that My children are living their lives in the truth. There is no music in Heaven that My angels can play, nor music on earth played by the greatest symphonic orchestra that has the melodious sound of this.

My Son, Jesus, is My New and Living Way. In the fullness of time I will reveal My Son in your children as I have promised I would do. They will look into His face and see My Love, My Forgiveness, My Mercy, My Longsuffering and My Patience towards them. They will say, " Father make me just like Jesus." I love to see your children trusting by faith for me to do just that. A lot of things in life bring me joy, but no greater joy than one life that discovers this truth and abides in My Grace. After all, this is what My Son, Jesus died for. The truth that sets your children free will enable them to daily walk in My Son, Jesus. I say there is no greater joy! This is My Covenant!

Enter Into My Joy

Well done My good and faithful servant, Enter into and share the joy of the Father. Matthew 24:21

In the beginning I spoke of My creation and said, "It is Good." I am Good. Only that which is created out of Me is good. I am the Good Shepherd and when I sent My perfect Lamb, Jesus, My spotless Lamb, My Son to be slain for your sin, I said "It is Good." I was well pleased. Out of that one sacrifice, My New Covenant could be brought in the earth to you and to your children and to your children's children forever for all eternity. When I sent Jesus, My angels proclaimed, "I bring you glad tidings of great joy!" In other words, Jesus is Good News!

Beloved, how lovely on the mountaintop are the feet of those who bring good news! As you have been on the mountaintop for many years and listened and sat in My presence, you have eaten My Word. With faith you have proclaimed in your heart, " Oh, this is good, this is so good." After our sweet communion together on the mountaintop, the natural everyday rigors of living are in the valley.

Satan, your adversary comes immediately to steal My Word which is sown in the heart. Your mind will always war and fight with that which is by faith in your heart. I told John when writing

Revelation that My Words would be sweet as honey in his mouth, but bitter to his belly. I had My angel offer him My Book, My Words and ask him to eat them. He could have refused. It is significant that John was told to take the book. It was not handed to him even when he asked the angel to give it to him, the reply was that he must take it himself.

Beloved, you must reach out and take the words of this Book yourself. Reach out, press in, and touch Me. Touch My Word, eat it, receive it. Situations will arise to work My Covenant in you in the valley of trial of everyday living. Share in my Son's sufferings, that even though My Words become bitter, My message will become a part of your life. It is good that we have fellowship daily in My Covenant.

Today satan waits to question all over again, "Did God really promise that you and your household shall be saved? Did He really say that to you?" He is always there, coming to steal and destroy My Word that I have given you. He is a liar and has been from the beginning. There is no truth in him. My Son's bride-to-be should not listen to another. My words always bring peace and comfort to your heart.

No greater joy exists than for you to live out your daily life in My Covenant. You may have bitter experiences in order for My Covenant to become an experiential part of your life. In doing this, you are saying to Me, your Father, "I trust you to bring forth this covenant in me and in My household."

My Son is making intercession for you. He is preparing a

house for you and your household. In the fullness of time, I will say to Him "Son, go get **her**---get the *joy* of your life! You counted her worth it all and you have kept your heart and eyes fixed upon **her**------

        THE
                "APPLE OF YOUR EYE"
                              AND MINE!

To order an additional copy of this book please complete the order form and mail it and a check to the following address:

His Love Publications
P.O. Box 5995
Thomasville, GA 31758

Name:_____

Address:_____

State:_____ Zip Code:_____

Telephone Number:_____

Number of books: ____ x $12.99 = _____

    Postage & Handling: 2.00

    $1.00 For each additional book: _____

    Add 5% Sales Tax: _____

    Check Amount: $ _____

Make Check or Money Order Payable to:
His Love Publications

To order an additional copy of this book please complete the order form and mail it and a check to the following address:

His Love Publications
P.O. Box 5995
Thomasville, GA 31758

Name:_____

Address:_____

State:_____ Zip Code:_____

Telephone Number:_____

Number of books: _____ x $12.99 = _____

   Postage & Handling: 2.00

   $1.00 For each additional book: _____

   Add 5% Sales Tax: _____

   Check Amount: $_____

Make Check or Money Order Payable to:
His Love Publications

To order an additional copy of this book please complete the order form and mail it and a check to the following address:

His Love Publications
P.O. Box 5995
Thomasville, GA 31758

Name:_____

Address:_____

State:_____ Zip Code:_____

Telephone Number:_____

Number of books: _____ x $12.99 = _____

    Postage & Handling: 2.00

    $1.00 For each additional book: _____

    Add 5% Sales Tax: _____

    Check Amount: $_____

Make Check or Money Order Payable to:
His Love Publications

To order an additional copy of this book please complete the order form and mail it and a check to the following address:

His Love Publications
P.O. Box 5995
Thomasville, GA 31758

Name:_____

Address:_____

State:_____ Zip Code:_____

Telephone Number:_____

Number of books: _____ x $12.99 = _____

    Postage & Handling: 2.00

    $1.00 For each additional book: _____

    Add 5% Sales Tax: _____

    Check Amount: $ _____

Make Check or Money Order Payable to:
His Love Publications

To order an additional copy of this book please complete the order form and mail it and a check to the following address:

His Love Publications
P.O. Box 5995
Thomasville, GA 31758

Name:_____

Address:_____

State:_____ Zip Code:_____

Telephone Number:_____

Number of books: ____ x $12.99 = _____

  Postage & Handling: 2.00

  $1.00 For each additional book: _____

  Add 5% Sales Tax: _____

  Check Amount: $ _____

Make Check or Money Order Payable to:
His Love Publications

To order an additional copy of this book please complete the order form and mail it and a check to the following address:

His Love Publications
P.O. Box 5995
Thomasville, GA 31758

Name:_____

Address:_____

State:_____ Zip Code:_____

Telephone Number:_____

Number of books: _____ x $12.99 = _____

    Postage & Handling: 2.00

    $1.00 For each additional book: _____

    Add 5% Sales Tax: _____

    Check Amount: $ _____

Make Check or Money Order Payable to:
His Love Publications